The Future of God

The Future of God

An Academic Perspective

STEPHEN R. SCHWALBE

WIPF & STOCK · Eugene, Oregon

THE FUTURE OF GOD
An Academic Perspective

Copyright © 2025 Stephen R. Schwalbe. All rights reserved. Except for brief quotations in critical publications or reviews, no part of this book may be reproduced in any manner without prior written permission from the publisher. Write: Permissions, Wipf and Stock Publishers, 199 W. 8th Ave., Suite 3, Eugene, OR 97401.

Wipf & Stock
An Imprint of Wipf and Stock Publishers
199 W. 8th Ave., Suite 3
Eugene, OR 97401

www.wipfandstock.com

PAPERBACK ISBN: 979-8-3852-4371-6
HARDCOVER ISBN: 979-8-3852-4372-3
EBOOK ISBN: 979-8-3852-4373-0

VERSION NUMBER 052925

All Scripture quotations are taken from the Holy Bible, New International Version®, NIV®. Copyright ©1973, 1978, 1984, 2011 by Biblica, Inc.™ Used by permission of Zondervan. All rights reserved worldwide. www.zondervan.com. The "NIV" and "New International Version" are trademarks registered in the United States Patent and Trademark Office by Biblica, Inc.™

I would like to dedicate this book
to the memory of my parents,
Richard W. Schwalbe and Gloria H. Schwalbe.

Contents

Figures | ix
Preface | xi
Acknowledgments | xiii
Introduction | xv

PART 1
Judaism | 9
Islam | 19
Christianity | 30
Evolution of God—Theology | 45
Evolution of God—Sociology | 55
Evolution of God—Biology | 74
Evolution of God—Physics | 77

PART 2
Future of God: It's Personal | 85
New, Revised God | 88
Evolution of Faith in God | 92
Accommodating a Personal God | 93

Conclusion | 98
Appendix | 101

Bibliography | 103
Index | 117
About the Author | 123

Figures

Figure 1: The Merneptah Stele | 10

Figure 2: Divided kingdoms—Israel and Judah | 13

Figure 3: Arabian Peninsula | 21

Figure 4: The Umayyad Caliphate, ca. 720 | 25

Figure 5: The Great Schism | 34

Figure 6: List of Crusades | 35

Figure 7: Map of Catholicism | 42

Figure 8: Founders of sociology | 57

Figure 9: Richard Dawkins | 75

Figure 10: Schema of recurring big bang and life cycles | 79

Figure 11: Stephen Hawking | 80

Preface

> The most vital concern for each of us is to have a joyful and fulfilled future.... Whatever people hope for in the future, that is what they worship, and whatever people worship, that is what they inevitably serve.
>
> —Daniel Fuller

This book completes a set of three books on religion. The first two books were inspired by the lack of publications on religion and conflict for a proposed elective class on this subject at the Air War College. As such, I authored two books: one focused on conflict related to the Abrahamic religions (Judaism, Christianity, and Islam) and the other on conflict related to the major Asian religions (Hinduism, Buddhism, and Shinto).[1] Now that these books are published, I wanted to complete this effort with a book oriented on the future of God.[2]

While there are many publications about the future of God or the future of religion, they tend to reflect a specific academic field, such as sociology or theology. In this book, I will review

---

1. *Killing for God* published in 2020 by Lexington Books and *Killing for Religion* published in 2022 by Resource Publications.

2. Note that each of the three books stands independent of one another. They are not a series.

the future of God reflected in various academic fields, including (in order) theology (dealing directly with God and religion), sociology (addressing how societies evolved with God and religion), biology (dealing with the scientific evidence of the existence of God), and physics (addressing God's intelligent design of the universe). Then, I will analyze each field's future projections for God to determine the most likely future or most likely combination. Finally, I will discuss a possible future religion based on the academic review about the future of God.

The question of the future of God was posed to the artificial intelligence program "Gemini." The AI response was as follows:

1. God is eternal and unchanging. This is the traditional theistic view.
2. God evolves with humanity. This is the process theology perspective.
3. The future of God is uncertain. This is the existentialist perspective.
4. The decline of religious belief. This is known as secularization.
5. The end of God. This is the nihilistic perspective.

I will discuss each of these perspectives in this book.

The book title refers to God and not religion primarily because God is associated with the Abrahamic religions, while religion encompasses all religions around the world. This book will focus on the future of God and not on the future of religion in general.

The audience for this book is not intended to be religious scholars. This book is oriented towards anyone generally interested in a potential future evolution of God, particularly those people who still attend church on a regular basis. It offers the perspective of several academic fields and an assessed direction based on the analysis of the information provided.

Acknowledgments

THIS BOOK DIRECTLY ADDRESSES the future of God based on an analysis of four academic fields including theology, sociology, biology, and physics. It reviews all three Abrahamic faiths (Judaism, Islam, and Christianity) to determine how humankind will accommodate God in the future.

I would like to thank Jim Bird; Steve Talmadge, PhD; Pastor Dave Johnson, PhD; and Pastor Matthew Erikson for reviewing my manuscript and offering me their keen insights.

I would like to express my heartfelt appreciation to the best copyeditor I have ever worked with: Hannah Starr. She was very thorough, as well as patient and understanding, throughout the editing process of my manuscript.

Finally, I would like to express my deepest appreciation to my wife, Ingrid, for all her assistance and support while I was researching and writing the manuscript.

Introduction

To BEGIN, LET'S DISCUSS the title of this book. I decided to explore the future of the more "developed" religions in the world today, meaning those with divine spirit(s), holy scriptures, established rituals, and global histories.[3] The Abrahamic religions (Judaism, Christianity, and Islam) are all monotheistic, believing in one God. They believe that God is all-knowing and all-powerful.[4] By referencing God in the title, I want readers to know that I intend on focusing only on the Abrahamic religions.

I focused primarily on Christianity in this book instead of Judaism or Islam. One reason is that it has more worldwide followers than the other two religions (at least for the near future, at 31 percent of the global population).[5] However, the primary reason is that Judaism and Islam are not evolving as Christianity is. As an example, when you search the Internet for the "future of Judaism" or "the future of Islam," all the hits are related to demographics, not theology or doctrine. The same is not the case for Christianity (which returns hits primarily related to demography but also nondemography as well). The main reason for this is that Judaism and Islam do not have formal mechanisms to allow for doctrinal changes like Christianity does.

  3. According to Stark, "No ancient civilizations possessed a truly coherent theology like that found in the Torah, Bible, or Qur'an." Stark, *Discovering God*, 78.
  4. Wright, *Evolution of God*, 21.
  5. Statistics and Data, "Major Religious Groups."

Introduction

A significant difference between Christianity and Judaism or Islam is that Christianity considers Jesus the Son of God, while the other two religions only recognize him as a prophet. As such, when he returned to heaven (i.e., the resurrection), plans were made to have a representative of Jesus on earth. According to Matt 16:18–19, before his resurrection Jesus conferred primacy upon Saint Peter to be the first bishop of Rome. This authority given by Christ to Saint Peter and his successors (known as popes) is called the primacy of Peter.

While the pope is human (hence, not perfect), the First Vatican Council (1869–1870) declared that the pope, when speaking on behalf of the church, is preserved from the possibility of error on doctrine. It does not mean the pope cannot sin or otherwise err in other situations. The doctrine of infallibility (i.e., papal supremacy) is a cornerstone of Catholic dogma, whereby the pope's authority determines what is accepted as Christian belief. Therefore, the pope has authority from God to change church doctrine and policy.[6] Except for Catholicism, every other Christian denomination evaluates what the pope decrees regarding their own religious beliefs. The bottom line is that Christianity has a more robust process and mechanism in place to evolve than Judaism or Islam.

---

6. Kirch, "Vatican Council."

PART 1

In the Beginning

Let's begin with attempting to define religion. Then, we can explore the origins of religion and examine its connection to myths. Additionally, the emergence of God will be discussed to prepare for the following academic section analyses.

Defining "religion" to accommodate all aspects of divine belief can be challenging. According to Alfred Whitehead, a former philosophy professor at Harvard University, "There is no agreement as to the definition of religion in its most general sense, including true and false religion; nor is there any agreement as to the valid religious beliefs, nor even as to what we mean by the truth of religion."[1] Nevertheless, he offered his own definition as one "whose beliefs and rituals have been reorganized with the aim of making it the central element in a coherent ordering of life—an ordering which shall be coherent both in respect to the elucidation of thought, and in respect to the direction of conduct towards a unified purpose commanding ethical approval."[2] Robert Bellah, a former professor of sociology at the University of California, Berkeley, defined religion as "a system of symbols that, when enacted by human beings, establishes powerful, pervasive, and long-lasting moods and

---

1. Whitehead, *Religion in the Making*, 14.
2. Whitehead, *Religion in the Making*, 15.

motivations that make sense in terms of an idea of a general order of existence."³ These definitions seem a bit broad, trending towards sociology and lacking any reference to a spiritual deity.

A couple of fundamental purposes for having any religion are that it gives people hope and comfort. These aspects of religion can be crucial for people's mental health. Kenneth Kardong, a former professor of zoology at Washington State University, noted, "Religion protects people from stress and the diseases related to it."⁴ It can also provide a sense of belonging and connection among people. According to Reza Aslan, a professor of theology at the University of California, Riverside, "The origins of religious impulse must be grounded in social life."⁵ It is likely that religion evolved to explain the natural world, particularly extraordinary weather phenomena, such as lightning and thunder, as well as to provide comfort and meaning to life. Early on, religion essentially served as the science explaining the physical world.⁶

Religious art and artifacts from ancient civilizations around the world support the belief that religion may have begun as early as the Middle Paleolithic era (three hundred thousand years ago). Religious symbols have been found in cave paintings and wall engravings.⁷

Religion has been a part of human societies from the beginning primarily because humans are psychologically primed for it.⁸ Religion evolved throughout history, from dominating early societies to becoming more of a spiritual reference in the modern world. Huston Smith, a renowned historian of religion who formerly taught at Washington University and the University of California, Berkeley, observed that "for the bulk of

3. Bellah, *Religion*, xiv.
4. Kardong, *Beyond God*, 123.
5. Aslan, *God*, 29.
6. Shelby, *Evolution*, 33.
7. FECYT Spanish Foundation, "Religious Beliefs."
8. Kardong, *Beyond God*, 124.

The Future of God—Part 1

human history, religion was lived in a tribal and virtually timeless mode."[9] In fact, throughout history, religion tends to be localized. Kardong wrote, "Over the long run, religious practices are present because they are adaptive behaviors suited to the local environment."[10]

While government did not evolve directly from religion, the two have often been closely linked. In the beginning, church and state were indistinguishable. According to Rodney Stark, a former sociology and comparative religion professor at the University of Washington, "In ancient civilizations, the concept of a 'state church' didn't really exist because people did not distinguish them as two institutions."[11] Bellah added, "In archaic societies, there is no such thing as religion or politics."[12]

Over time, church and state separated by different degrees depending on the society. In Europe during the seventeenth century, this separation became pronounced due to the efforts of Roger Williams and John Locke. Williams was a Protestant minister who founded the Plymouth Plantations in 1636 (which became the colony of Rhode Island). He was the first to advocate for a wall of separation between the church and state. John Locke, an English philosopher and physician, argued in *A Letter Concerning Toleration* (1685) that the proper realm of government concerns "civil interests." He advocated that the government's concerns should extend only to civil matters and not to religious affairs, while the church's concerns should focus on spiritual affairs and not civil matters.[13]

With so many different religions around the world, they cannot all be true. What is true is that the followers of a specific religion have faith that their religion is valid regardless of any other religion's beliefs. (That is human nature.)

9. Smith, *World's Religions*, xiii.
10. Kardong, *Beyond God*, 150.
11. Stark, *Discovering God*, 101.
12. Bellah, *Religion*, 236.
13. Tuckness, "Locke's Political Philosophy," §7.

The Future of God—Part 1

One of the earliest identified religions is animism. Animism means "breath, spirit, life" in Latin.[14] Followers of animism believe that a supernatural power animates the universe and that all objects and creatures possess a divine essence. According to Aslan, "The ancient societies worshipped the spirits that resided in objects, like stones."[15]

A variation of animism is Shinto, the indigenous religion of Japan. *Kami* is a Japanese term that pertains to a god, spirit, or spirituality. Kami can take the form of things like rocks, rivers, and stars, as well as aspects of nature, such as rain and sunshine. Shinto holds that kami can influence human events and the forces of nature.[16] Let's now turn to how myths affect religion.

Myths

Whitehead defined *myth* as follows:

> A myth will involve special attention to some persons or to some things, real or imaginary.... A myth satisfies the demands of incipient rationality. Men found themselves practicing various rituals, and found the rituals generating emotions. The myth explains the purpose both of the ritual and of the emotion. It is the product of the vivid fancy of primitive men in an unfathomed world.[17]

Karen Armstrong, a religious scholar and author, offered her insights into myths, stating, "From the very beginning, human beings have been myth-makers. We are meaning-seeking creatures and perpetually create mythologies to explain our circumstances, especially when we are in distress."[18] However,

---

14. Segal, *Myth*, 14; Stringer, "Rethinking Animism"; Hornborg, "Animism"; Haught, *What Is Religion?*, 19; Van Eyghen, "Animism".
15. Aslan, *God*, 78.
16. World Religions, "Shintoism."
17. Whitehead, *Religion in the Making*, 24.
18. Armstrong, *Role of Religion*, 4.

Bellah cautioned, "Myths are inherently unreliable because they recount stories that are handed down orally and occurred so far in the past that no one can possibly know if they are true or not."[19]

As part of the evolution of religion in ancient times, myths were usually passed orally from generation to generation. Smith wrote that "myths are the language of religion."[20] Michael Coogan, a former professor of religious studies at Stonehill College and a lecturer on the Old Testament / Hebrew Bible at Harvard Divinity School, offered his insights into biblical myths: "In its simplest sense, a myth is a narrative—the Greek word *mythos* originally meant story—in either prose or poetry, in which gods and goddesses are the principal characters. Although people sometimes find the idea shocking, the Old Testament is also imbued with myth."[21] According to Stark, most myths are not included in scriptures as they do not expound religious doctrine. Instead, they serve to illustrate values and beliefs.[22] He cited the ancient great flood as an example of a shared historical global myth found in cultures from the Middle East to the Māori of New Zealand. Indigenous versions of a flood epic can be found in Egypt, Babylon, Greece, India, Europe, East Asia, North and South America, and Australia.[23] The *Epic of Gilgamesh*, the greatest of ancient Mesopotamian poems, is important as a myth because it explores the themes of mortality and friendship. The poem also provides insights into the ancient Mesopotamian world and its culture.[24]

There are many notable myths in both the Old and New Testaments of the Bible.[25] The Old Testament is a collection of

19. Bellah, *Religion*, 390.
20. Smith, *Why Religion Matters*, 30.
21. Coogan, *Old Testament*, 33.
22. Stark, *Discovering God*, 86.
23. Stark, *Discovering God*, 88.
24. Bellah, *Religion*, 224.
25. Mostert, *God*, 73.

historical myths written over centuries by numerous authors. Some well-known myths in the Old Testament include the creation story (God created the world in six days), the fall of man (Eve ate the forbidden fruit in the garden of Eden), the aforementioned flood story (Noah and his ark), the Tower of Babel (multiple languages of the people building a tower to heaven), the binding of Isaac (God commanded Abraham to sacrifice his son), and the exodus story (Moses led the Israelites out of Egypt to the promised land). These stories are important because they provide insights into the beliefs and values of the ancient Israelites, who likely adopted them from the Chaldeans and Babylonians before them.[26] Even our present notion of hell does not come from the Bible but from pagan philosophy, myths, and literature (e.g., Dante's *Inferno*).[27]

The myths present in the Hebrew Bible are likely taken from earlier Mesopotamian legends.[28] Much of the Hebrew Bible is similar or identical to other Near Eastern peoples' myths, legends, folktales, and poetry. For example, the story of Moses is similar to the story of Sargon the Great, and the flood legend (described in Genesis) is likely taken from the *Epic of Gilgamesh*.[29]

In the New Testament, the most important myth is the resurrection of Jesus following his crucifixion (note: crucifixion and resurrection accounts were common during the time of Jesus[30]). Other important myths included the virgin birth of Jesus (at that time, "virgin" meant a young woman—Mary was probably fifteen or sixteen years old when she birthed Jesus[31]),

---

26. NSCC, "Hebrews."

27. Evely, *End of Ages*, 45.

28. It was in Mesopotamia that gods first entered the historical record. Gods were seen as humans with supernatural powers. Wright, *Evolution of God*, 70.

29. NSCC, "Hebrews."

30. Galbraith, "When Jesus Was Alive."

31. Andrews, "How Old Was Mary."

the ascension of Jesus into heaven, and the second coming of Jesus. Over time, new myths were promulgated in the Christian faith, such as Jesus being the Son of God and the existence of the Holy Spirit (neither concept, as they are understood today, is mentioned in the Bible).[32] As such, it can be alleged that the Bible is a compendium of historical myths.[33] Next, let's review how God may have been created.

God Is a Human Creation

Essentially, "God" is humankind's greatest invention (not fire, the wheel, or beer). In fact, Voltaire, a famous French philosopher, alluded to this, stating, "If God did not exist, it would be necessary to invent him."[34] Aslan noted, "God is a divine version of ourselves."[35] As humankind has evolved over the millennia, so has our perception of God, as reflected in religious doctrine, rituals, and myths.[36] Aslan concluded, "As politics on earth changed, the politics of heaven changed to match."[37] In fact, the author Alex Shelby determined that religion's characteristics closely resemble something man-made.[38]

As humankind made advances, religion evolved accordingly. Regarding this correlation, Stephen Sanderson, a former

---

32. According to Sanderson, neither Jesus nor his followers saw him as the Son of God. Sanderson, *Religious Evolution*, 71.

33. Some scholars say the Bible is a collection of stories and myths recorded by many authors over a period of up to sixteen hundred years. The Bible is an anthology of texts written in Hebrew, Aramaic, and Greek that includes instructions, stories, poetry, and prophecies. Shelby claimed the Bible is outdated, having been revised and even forged. Shelby, *Evolution*, 60.

34. Socratic Method, "Voltaire."

35. Aslan, *God*, xiii.

36. This perception never explained the nature of God or the five mass extinctions the earth has witnessed.

37. Aslan, *God*, 104.

38. Shelby, *Evolution*, 6. The evolution of religion reveals a strong correlation with the evolution of government.

visiting sociology scholar at the University of California, Riverside, observed, "Advances in subsistence economy, increases in population, and the development of writing and record keeping were necessary conditions for religious evolution over the long run."[39] Many scholars believe that God only exists in the human imagination. As such, gods around the world share many human characteristics. Stark pointed out, "Most Gods looked like human beings, and all had human desires and defects."[40]

W. Jay Wood, a former professor of philosophy at Wheaton College, believes that the world's religions say incompatible things about God such that consensus about who God is appears unattainable.[41] The bottom line is that as a nation's culture changes, so does the perception of God and the purpose of religion. As there are numerous cultures around the world, it would be impossible to reach a consensus about who God has been, is today, or will be in the future. In addition, the fact that there are so many similarities among the world's religions is additional evidence that they are human inventions.

Up to now, we have briefly reviewed the origins of religion, the myths involved in the evolution of religion, and the nature of God. The key question for the next part of this book is which of the Abrahamic religions can best determine the future of God? As such, it is useful to briefly review the histories of the three Abrahamic religions to see how each evolved to its present state and to determine what the future is for Yahweh/Allah/God.

---

39. Sanderson, *Religious Evolution*, 190.
40. Stark, *Discovering God*, 77.
41. Wood, *God*, 190.

Judaism

THE HISTORY OF JUDAISM is essentially that of the Jewish people. Jews are an ethnoreligious group originating from the Hebrews (a.k.a. Israelites) of the historical kingdoms of Israel and Judah. Jewish religion, ethnicity, and nationhood are strongly interrelated. Jewish culture includes a language (Hebrew), a shared history, and an attachment to land that was once known as Canaan. Geographically, Canaan was fairly unimpressive. It was a relatively small region with few natural resources or geographic highlights.[1]

In general, the beginning of the Jewish people began sometime after 3000 BCE. By 3000 BCE, Egypt already had its grand pyramids, and Sumer and Akkadia were world empires. Overall, Jewish history is relatively insignificant when compared with the histories of Babylon, Egypt, and Syria.[2]

Jewish History

To begin, the Jewish people were first identified in Canaan in the Levant region (known today as Israel) during the late second millennium BCE. An inscription on the Merneptah Stele

---

1. Smith, *World's Religions*, 312; Mark, "Canaan."
2. Smith, *World's Religions*, 271–72.

appears to confirm the existence of Jewish people there as far back as the thirteenth century BCE.[3]

Figure 1: The Merneptah Stele is an inscription by Merneptah, an Egyptian pharaoh who ruled from 1213 to 1203 BCE. It represents the earliest reference to Israel.[4]

God selected Abraham to be the father of the Jewish people.[5] God promised Abraham that Isaac, his second son, would become ruler of Canaan. However, Jews did not conquer Canaan, as commonly thought, but rather settled there peacefully among the Canaanites.[6] Later, the descendants of Isaac's first son, Jacob, were enslaved in Egypt when looking for food during a drought. Enslaved people did most of the manual labor

---

3. World History Edu, "Merneptah Stele."

4. Photograph of Merneptah Stele courtesy of Onceinawhile, CC BY-SA 4.0 (https://creativecommons.org/licenses/by-sa/4.0/), Wikimedia Commons.

5. Smith, *World's Religions*, 284.

6. Bellah, *Religion*, 287.

Judaism

performed in Egypt, including the Jews. In Exod 3:7–10, God commanded Moses to lead the exodus of the Jews out of Egypt.[7]

According to Hebrew Scriptures, the twelve sons of Jacob collectively formed the Israelite nation around this time. Modern scholars doubt that there were precisely twelve Israelite tribes. (It is believed that numerology in the Middle East considers the number twelve to represent a "complete set.") Bellah, for example, believes this is simply another myth.[8]

At Mount Sinai, the Hebrews received the *Torah*—the five books of Moses.[9] Initially, the Jewish nation had no kings, as they followed the Torah and the guidance of *Yahweh* (their God).[10] In the beginning, the Israelites were led by priests, prophets, and judges. The priests and prophets relayed the word of Yahweh, while the judges advised the people in times of peace and led them in times of war. Then in 880 BCE, after four hundred years of being led by this group of Jewish leaders, the people approached the prophet Samuel, asking specifically for a king.[11] So, Samuel anointed Saul to be their first king.[12] Eventually, Saul disobeyed Yahweh and Samuel by not exterminating the

---

7. "The LORD said, 'I have indeed seen the misery of my people in Egypt. I have heard them crying out because of their slave drivers, and I am concerned about their suffering. So I have come down to rescue them from the hand of the Egyptians and to bring them up out of that land into a good and spacious land, a land flowing with milk and honey—the home of the Canaanites, Hittites, Amorites, Perizzites, Hivites and Jebusites. And now the cry of the Israelites has reached me, and I have seen the way the Egyptians are oppressing them. So now, go. I am sending you to Pharaoh to bring my people the Israelites out of Egypt" (Exod 3:7–10).

8. Bellah, *Religion*, 286.

9. According to Sanderson, Moses did not write the Torah. Sanderson, *Religious Evolution*, 69.

10. Yahweh was originally one of many Canaanite gods but eventually was elevated to be the supreme god. Sanderson, *Religious Evolution*, 66; Wright, *Evolution of God*, 123.

11. Posner, "Hebrew Monarchy."

12. "When Samuel heard all that the people said, he repeated it before the LORD. The LORD answered, 'Listen to them and give them a king'" (1 Sam 8:21–22).

inhabitants of Canaan. As a result, Samuel replaced him with David.[13]

Solomon, King David's son, built the first temple in Jerusalem. After Solomon's death, in 975 BCE, there was a conflict among the tribes involving taxation. As a result, the nation split into two kingdoms: the kingdom of Israel, with its capital at Samaria, and the kingdom of Judah, with its capital in Jerusalem. The kingdom of Israel was eventually destroyed by the Neo-Assyrian Empire around 722 BCE, and its people were deported. The kingdom of Judah was subsequently defeated by the Neo-Babylonian Empire in 586 BCE. Unfortunately, Jerusalem and the first temple were destroyed as a result. The Judeans were exiled to Babylon as slaves. In 539 BCE, Cyrus the Great of the Persian Empire conquered Babylon. He ordered Jerusalem to be rebuilt along with the second temple. Cyrus allowed the Judeans to return to their homeland in 538 BCE—an event known as the "return to Zion."[14]

---

13. "Because you have rejected the word of the Lord, he has rejected you as king" (1 Sam 15:23); Kohler, "Israel."

14. Posner, "Hebrew Monarchy."

Figure 2: Divided kingdoms—Israel and Judah[15]

After several centuries of foreign rule, the Jews revolted against the Greek Seleucid Empire in what came to be known as the Maccabean Revolt (167–160 BCE). The revolt stemmed from Jewish opposition to severe Greek repression. In 164 BCE, a group of Jewish warriors called the Maccabees captured Jerusalem. Simon Thassi, the leader of the Maccabees, then

---

15. "Kingdoms of Israel and Judah Map 830" courtesy of Malus Catulus, CC BY-SA 3.0 (https://creativecommons.org/licenses/by-sa/3.0/), Wikimedia Commons.

established the Hasmonean Dynasty in 141 BCE.[16] A civil war between brothers in 63 BCE led to the demise of the dynasty and to the Romans being invited to get involved in the region.[17]

Zealots were essentially Jewish freedom fighters (or terrorists, from the Roman perspective) who sought to overthrow the subsequent Roman rule in Jerusalem. The Zealots led a major uprising in 66 CE and expelled the Romans from Jerusalem. Eventually, the Romans returned to defeat the Zealots in 73 CE, known as the "Great Revolt." Roman Emperor Hadrian punished the Jewish people by building a pagan idol on the ruins of the Temple Mount.[18] Roman oppression of the Jewish population eventually provoked another revolt, known as the Bar Kokhba Revolt (132–136 CE). After the Romans suppressed this revolt, they outlawed Jews from practicing their faith altogether.[19]

In 629 CE, the Roman Emperor Heraclius I drove the Jewish people from Jerusalem and killed Jews throughout the empire. Meanwhile, Muslim forces attacked Egypt and laid siege to Alexandria in 640 CE. After the city fell, the Treaty of Alexandria stipulated that the Jewish residents would be allowed to remain in Alexandria unmolested. After the final Muslim conquest of Egypt in 969 CE by the Fatimid dynasty, Jews from all over North Africa resettled there.[20]

Between the twelfth and fifteenth centuries, Jews experienced persecution in Central Europe which caused many of them to migrate to Eastern Europe. In 1492 CE, Jews were forced to leave Spain when the government enforced the Alhambra

---

16. Oates, "Maccabean Revolt."
17. Wein, "End of the Hasmoneans."
18. Jewish Virtual Library, "Great Revolt."
19. Jewish Virtual Library, "Bar-Kokhba Revolt."
20. Butler, *Arab Conquest*, 311–30. The Fatimid dynasty ruled from 909–1171 CE. The Fatimids were a Muslim Shia clan.

Decree to eliminate unwanted Jewish influence. They migrated in great numbers to the Ottoman Empire.[21]

In the late nineteenth century, Jews in Europe faced growing persecution, legal restrictions, and widespread hostilities. Between 1881 and 1924, violent attacks against the Jews triggered a mass exodus of Jews worldwide. During this time, Jews began a movement to reestablish a Jewish state in Palestine. This Zionist movement was founded in 1897 by Theodor Herzl, a Jewish lawyer.[22]

By 1933, the situation in Germany became very difficult for the Jewish population once the Nazis and their leader, Adolph Hitler, assumed political power. Anti-Semitic laws continued to be promulgated in Germany during the 1930s, leading to enormous numbers of Jews leaving the country primarily for the United States, the Soviet Union, and Palestine. In 1941, Hitler began the implementation of the "Final Solution"—the extermination of all Jewish people under Nazi control. Around six million Jews were killed during this program, known today as the Holocaust.[23]

On May 14, 1948, after the United Nations General Assembly approved the creation of the State of Israel, David Ben-Gurion declared Israel an independent country. Immediately afterward, the neighboring Arab states attacked Israel. In 1949, the Israeli military defeated this Arab alliance, and the United Nations brokered a peace settlement. Subsequently, Israel began receiving Jews from all over the world.[24] As of 2024, Israel is a parliamentary democracy with a population of 9.6 million people.[25]

---

21. Brinkmann, "Jewish Migration."
22. Holocaust Memorial Museum, "Holocaust Survivors."
23. Library of Congress, "From Haven to Home"; Holocaust Memorial Museum, "Holocaust Survivors."
24. Office of the Historian, "Arab-Israeli War."
25. *BBC News*, "Israel Country Profile."

The Future of God—Part 1

History of Judaism

The earliest text of Judaism is the Hebrew Bible (also known as the Tanakh). It is a collection of twenty-four books written in Hebrew and Aramaic over a period of one thousand years (1500–400 BCE).[26] This text is the basis for the religious beliefs and practices of the Jewish people. Its teachings have been passed down from generation to generation and are still studied and practiced today. However, much of the Hebrew Bible was adopted from the religions of other ancient civilizations—a process known as syncretism. Andrew White, cofounder and former president of Cornell University, along with many other religious scholars, believes that most (if not all) of the myths, legends, and traditions cited in the Hebrew Bible come from Chaldea, Babylonia, and Assyria. According to White,

> Assyrian inscriptions . . . show that in the ancient religions of Chaldea and Babylonia there was elaborated a narrative of the creation which must have been the source of that in our own sacred books. It has now become clear that from the same sources which inspired the accounts of the creation of the universe among Chaldeo-Babylonian, the Assyrian, the Phoenician, and other ancient civilizations came the ideas which hold so prominent a place in the sacred books of the Hebrews.[27]

The Hebrew Bible is divided into three sections: the Torah (allegedly written by Moses), the Prophets (earlier and later), and the Writings.[28] The Torah consists of the five books of Moses: Genesis, Exodus, Leviticus, Numbers, and Deuteronomy. The Greek name for this group of five books is the *Pentateuch*. The Pentateuch provides the context of Jewish laws and traditions.[29]

---

26. Parrinder, *World Religions*, 385.
27. White, *History of the Warfare*, ch. 1, part 1.
28. Parrinder, *World Religions*, 401, 385.
29. Goodfriend, "Why Is the Torah Divided."

Judaism

A common myth is that Moses was given the Torah directly from God at Mount Sinai and in the tabernacle. Bellah noted that much of Moses' story comes from Assyrian sources.[30] Most modern scholars say that the Torah's compilation results from editing done over the years by many scribes, with the final editing occurring around 539 BCE when Cyrus the Great conquered the Babylonian Empire.[31]

Then, there is the *Talmud*, a collection of history, law, folklore, and rabbinic commentary that is the basis of Judaism. The Talmud is considered an oral tradition that explains the written texts of the Torah so that people would know how to apply them to their lives.[32] The Talmud has two parts: the *Mishnah* (Judaism's first written Oral Law) and the *Gemara* (writings about the Hebrew Bible). Additionally, there are two versions of the Talmud: the Babylonian Talmud (the most widely used one) and the Jerusalem Talmud (the oldest one dating back to the eighth century CE).[33]

According to the Talmud, the men of the Great Assembly compiled and canonized much of the Hebrew Bible, a task completed in 400 BCE.[34] It has remained unchanged since then (over two thousand years). The Great Assembly, also known as the Great Synagogue, was established by Ezra the scribe and consisted of a hundred and twenty prophets, sages, and scribes.[35]

In the Hebrew Bible, God is referred to as *Yahweh*. Yahweh was the God of the kingdoms of Israel and Judah. Yahweh is regarded as the highest God and serves as the foundation of Judaism.[36] Yahweh is a God of righteousness whose loving-

---

30. Bellah, *Religion*, 309.
31. Berlin, *Poetics and Interpretation*, 113.
32. Smith, *World's Religions*, 313.
33. New World Encyclopedia, "Talmud."
34. Faithful Version, "Canonization."
35. Jewish History, "Great Assembly."
36. Smith, *World's Religions*, 176; Bellah, *Religion*, 295.

kindness is everlasting.[37] As such, Judaism affirms the world's goodness. From the account in Gen 1:1–10, "In the beginning, God created the heavens and the earth. . . .And God saw that it was *good*" (Gen 1:1, 10; emphasis mine).

On the other hand, in the same Hebrew Bible, Yahweh is depicted as violent, coercive, punishing, threatening, and deadly, as demonstrated by the extraordinary violence displayed through genocidal floods, plagues, and military triumphs. The exodus myth was a story of God's liberating violence, while the exile myth was a story of God's punishing violence. As such, regarding Yahweh, obey him and be blessed, or disobey him and be punished.[38]

Not much has changed in Judaism over the past two thousand years, as there are no formal mechanisms or processes to accommodate any changes. In fact, recent trends have stressed strict conformity to the Torah and Talmud. This is referred to as the Jewish fundamentalist movement. Today, there are two primary fundamentalist movements in Judaism: Zionism and the ultra-Orthodox.[39]

---

37. Smith, *World's Religions*, 275.
38. Nelson-Pallmeyer, *Is Religion Killing Us?*, 28–51.
39. Shanes, "Jewish Denominations."

Islam

History

Islam originated in Mecca and Medina on the Arabian Peninsula in the early seventh century, with the Prophet Muhammad as its founder and champion. Muhammad was born into the respectable Hashim family in Mecca in 570 CE. Abdullah ibn Abd al-Muttalib was his father and Amina bint Wahb was his mother. Unfortunately, Abdullah died a few months before Muhammad's birth and Amina died when he was only six years old. As a result, Muhammad was raised by his grandfather, Abd al-Muttalib, and his paternal uncle, Abu Talib.[1]

Muhammad's family was part of the Quraysh clan, the most powerful clan in Mecca at that time. As he grew up, Muhammad spent a lot of time visiting with transient traders coming to Mecca, a regional trading center.[2] He was most likely aware of Jewish beliefs and practices from them and the religious pilgrims visiting Mecca. As a result of learning about Judaism, it is possible that the monotheistic teachings of Abraham, Moses, and Jesus inspired Muhammad.

When he was forty years old (in 610 CE), he told his friends and family that he was visited by the archangel Gabriel

---

1. Philosopher, "Muhammad"; Timmons, "Muhammad."
2. Philosopher, "Muhammad."

in a nearby cave on Mount Jabal al-Nour (called Hira) where he regularly meditated and prayed. During subsequent visits, Gabriel revealed insights from Allah (the Arabic word for God) to Muhammad. Muhammad could not read or write but was able to repeat what Gabriel had told him to his family and friends, who then wrote it down. These visits continued for the rest of Muhammad's life. By 613 CE, Muhammad began preaching publicly about the rich giving to the poor and abandoning idolatry. He also promoted the foundations of Islam (i.e., that "Allah is One," that "submission" to Allah is the right way of life, and that he was a prophet and messenger of Allah) among the people of Mecca.[3]

Muhammad's beliefs threatened the Meccan polytheists who then began to attack him, his family, and his followers for over a dozen years (one reason for Muhammad to spend a lot of time in the cave). In 619 CE, after he lost protection with the death of his uncle, Abu Talib, Muhammad moved from Mecca to Medina, a city over two hundred miles to the northeast. In 622 CE, his family and followers joined him there.[4] By 629 CE, Muhammad united the various clans (who were constantly fighting one another) under the Constitution of Medina. He eventually became the mayor of Medina. The Medina clans fought off and on with the Meccan clans for almost a decade. Finally, Muhammad assembled an army of ten thousand Muslim converts, and in 630 CE, he successfully attacked and conquered Mecca.[5]

Muhammad likely caught pleurisy during his farewell pilgrimage to Mount Arafat in 632 CE. He died within a few months at the age of sixty-two (an elder statesman in those days). At the time of his passing, most of the Arabian Peninsula had been conquered by Muhammad's army and converted to Islam. It is important to note that two important political

---

3. Philosopher, "Muhammad."

4. This event marks the beginning of the Islamic calendar and is called the Hijrah. Philosopher, "Muhammad."

5. Philosopher, "Muhammad."

traditions in Islam evolved during Muhammad's life—Muhammad as a rebel, in Mecca; and Muhammad as a statesman, in Medina.[6]

Figure 3: Arabian Peninsula[7]

When Muhammad died, there was significant disagreement over who would succeed him as leader of the Arab Muslims. The problem was that Muhammad died without designating a male heir or establishing a mechanism to replace him. Most of Muhammad's followers thought that according to ancient Arab tradition and culture, Islamic community elders would choose his successor (Sunni Muslims). However, a minority group believed that only a blood relative from Muhammad's family could succeed him (in this case, his cousin and

---

6. Philosopher, "Muhammad."

7. "Saudi Arabia Map" courtesy of NormanEinstein, CC BY-SA 3.0 (https://creativecommons.org/licenses/by-sa/3.0/), Wikimedia Commons.

The Future of God—Part 1

son-in-law, Ali ibn Abi Talib). This group became known as the followers of Ali (Shi'a Muslims).[8]

Umar ibn al-Khattab, Muhammad's prominent companion, recommended that Abu Bakr, Muhammad's friend and close collaborator, become the first caliph. And Abu Bakr was eventually confirmed as such.[9] (The office of the caliph retained an aura of authority much like that of the Catholic pope, but not the same. While the pope is perceived to be God's representative on earth, the caliph serves as the political and religious leader of the Muslim world.)

As such, a great schism began between Sunni and Shi'a factions. Muhammad had created a Muslim state on the Arabian Peninsula where various tribes paid alms, taxes, and tributes to him, known as *zakat*. This combination of money and power would grow exponentially over time. However, many tribal leaders subsequently refused to deal with Abu Bakr, including not making the zakat payments.[10]

During his reign, Caliph Abu Bakr consolidated and expanded the rule of the Muslim state over the entire Arabian Peninsula. His rule was immediately tested by apostates (people who resisted Islam) in a series of uprisings known as the Ridda wars (632–633 CE). These rebellions threatened the unity and stability of the newly formed Islamic state but were eventually defeated. After reuniting the Arabs, Abu Bakr launched successful invasions into neighboring Syria and Iraq in 633 CE.[11]

Abu Bakr is also credited with compiling the first Qur'an. Additionally, to avoid any succession issues, Abu Bakr nominated his principal adviser, Umar ibn al-Khattab, to be his successor before dying of natural causes in 634 CE.[12]

---

8. Sowerwine, "Caliph and Caliphate."
9. Khan, "Umar."
10. Quranic Education, "Abu Bakr."
11. World History Edu, "Abu Bakr."
12. World History Edu, "Abu Bakr."

Islam

The Sunni tribal elders agreed that Umar should succeed Abu Bakr as the second caliph. Umar was the father-in-law and close companion of the Prophet Muhammad. During his reign, he improved the administration of the Muslim empire and introduced a judicial system, law enforcement, and state treasury (known as Bayt al Mal).[13]

From the beginning, Muslims set for themselves the task of spreading Islam across the entire planet. By the end of Umar's rule, Egypt, Syria, and much of Persia were incorporated into the Muslim world.[14] During the seventh century, Muslims won a religious war in the Near East between Christians (believers in the Trinity), Zoroastrians (believers in dualism—good versus evil[15]), and Islam (believers in Allah).[16]

In 644 CE, Umar was stabbed by a Persian Christian slave and died from his wounds. Uthman ibn Affan, Muhammad's second cousin and son-in-law, was selected to be the third caliph, as prearranged. Caliph Uthman directed that the Qur'an be compiled using a standardized dialect (i.e., Qurayshi Arabic). Once this was completed (between 650 and 656 CE), then copies were disseminated throughout the Muslim empire. Under his administration, numerous public welfare projects were completed.[17]

When rebels killed Uthman while praying in his home in 656 CE, Ali ibn Abi Ṭalib, cousin and son-in-law of Muhammad, finally became the caliph—as initially advocated by the Shia faction. He subsequently moved the caliphate capital to Kufa. Ali ordered a standardized copy of the Qur'an to be prepared to account for the missing vowels in the written Arabic language (potentially causing interpretation issues). In 661 CE,

13. Khan, "Umar."
14. Partner, *God of Battles*, 38.
15. Zoroastrianism was the first monotheistic religion. Sanderson, *Religious Evolution*, 56.
16. Aslan, *God*, 147–49.
17. Khan, "Umar"; Mamun, "Hazrat Uthman Ibn Affan."

Ali was assassinated by a Kharijite, a fundamentalist sect, possibly seeking revenge for their defeat at the Battle of Nahrawa in 658 CE.[18]

Ali's firstborn son, and the grandson of the Prophet Muhammad, Hasan ibn Ali, became caliph six months after the assassination. Unfortunately, Muawiyah I was the governor of Syria, and he refused to acknowledge Hasan as the new caliph. As such, Hasan led a military force to defeat Muawiyah I, but was unsuccessful due in part to the high number of defections from his army. At this point, Hasan negotiated a peace treaty with Marwan I in which he would step aside to live quietly in Medina with a generous pension. In 670 CE, Hasan, who was forty-six years old at the time, was poisoned to death by one of his wives, who was close to Muawiyah I.[19]

Hussain ibn Ali, Hasan's brother and Muhammad's only surviving grandson, refused to swear allegiance to Yazid, the current Umayyad caliph, because he was Shia and not Sunni. Hussain, along with seventy-two family members and loyal friends, were killed in the Battle of Karbala in 680 CE.[20]

Muslim rule was expanded under Marwan I (see figure 4). At its height, the Umayyad dynasty became one of the largest empires in world history, covering more than five million square miles.[21]

---

18. Alim, "Kharijite Plot"; Islamic Finder, "Short Biography."

19. Encyclopedia Britannica, "Hasan."

20. Who Is Hussain, "Full Story of Hussain." This battle is now commemorated as the Day of Ashura. StudyCorgi, "Sunni and Shia' Branches."

21. Blankinship, *End of the Jihad State*, 37; History Guild, "Umayyad and Abbasid Empire."

Islam

Figure 4: The Umayyad Caliphate, ca. 720[22]

Alongside the territorial growth of the Umayyad Caliphate, the sectarian split between Sunni and Shia Muslims eventually became violent again. However, the Sunni sect emerged as dominant in most regions of the Muslim world, except for Iran, Iraq, Azerbaijan, Bahrain, and Lebanon.[23]

As the Umayyad empire grew, the state expenses increased.[24] With its immense wealth, the Umayyad rule was perceived as contrary to the Islamic message preached by the Prophet Muhammad. This wealth and subsequent corruption increased discontent among the Muslim people. The descendants of Muhammad's uncle Abbas ibn Abd al-Muttalib organized discontented *mawali* (freed slaves and non-Arab Muslims) and some Shia to rise against the Umayyads. In 750 CE, they were successful and inaugurated the Abbasid dynasty,

---

22. Image of Umayyad Caliphate map courtesy of Ergovius, CC BY-SA 4.0 (https://creativecommons.org/licenses/by-sa/4.0/), Wikimedia Commons.

23. StudyCorgi, "Sunni and Shia' Branches."

24. Khan, "Umayyad Dynasty."

with its capital in Baghdad. Although most of the Umayyad family were killed, one family member, Abd al-Rahman I, escaped to Spain and established the Caliphate of Córdoba in 756 CE. It lasted until 1031 CE when it collapsed due to civil war.[25]

Under the Abbasids, Islamic civilization experienced its "golden age." Advances were made in commerce, astronomy, literature, arts, philosophy, industry, science, and mathematics. Additionally, the capital was moved from Damascus to Baghdad to allow the Abbasid elites to better engage with Persia. The Abbasid caliphs drew heavily upon the traditions of the Persian and Byzantine empires that preceded them.[26]

With such a large and diverse empire, political problems were likely to occur. Eventually, the Abbasids became involved in disputes among Coptic Arab, Indo-Persian, and Turkish factions. In this case, the Arabs and Turks were Sunni Muslims, while the Indo-Persians were Shia Muslims. At this point, the unity of the Abbasid dynasty and the Muslim world began to disintegrate. Adding to the political turmoil was economic stress due to the immense costs to run the empire, and the mismanagement of funds.[27]

By 945 CE, the Abbasid Caliphate began to fall apart as minor dynasties, including the Tahirid, Saffarids, Samanids, and the Ghaznavids, took hold and grew. By 1055 CE, the emerging Seljuk Empire (a Sunni Turkish clan) assumed control of the Abbasid Caliphate.[28]

Meanwhile, the Asian Mongol Empire had conquered most of Persia and Afghanistan. Then, it turned its attention to the Middle East. Under the leadership of Genghis Khan, the Mongol hordes razed Baghdad to the ground in 1258 CE, thus

---

25. Corcuera, "Abbasid Revolution"; Khan, "Abbasid Dynasty."
26. Hurst, "Abbasid Caliphate."
27. Nasr, *Islam*, 121–22; Lapidus, *History of Islamic Societies*, 129.
28. Chakra, "Rise and Fall."

destroying what was left of the Abbasid Caliphate. (In total, the Abbasids reigned from 750 to 1258 CE.)[29]

The Fatimid Dynasty began in Tunisia in 909 CE. It expanded and conquered Egypt by 969 CE. The Fatimid Dynasty became one of the largest Muslim empires ever, but it ended peacefully with the beginning of the Ayyubid Sultanate in Egypt in 1171 CE.[30]

In 1250 CE, the Mamluk Sultanate was created after it defeated the Ayyubid Sultanate. The Mamluks were former slaves that embraced a warrior culture. This culture gave the Mamluks the edge needed to successfully confront the Mongol Empire during its invasions of the Middle East. The Mongol invaders were finally stopped by the Mamluks north of Jerusalem in 1260 CE at the Battle of Ain Jalut. A few months later, the Mongols were defeated again by the Mamluks at the Battle of Homs. With this, the Mamluks repelled the Mongol invasion and were able to control the entire Levant region.[31]

In 1295 CE, a Buddhist named Mahmud Ghazan became Khan of the Mongolian Empire. He subsequently converted to Islam and then compelled other Mongol notables to follow suit. Prior to the Mongol conversion to Islam, Mongol invasions (along with those of Tamerlane from the East) were generally successful against the Muslim armies.[32]

The Mongols not only instilled terror among the conquered societies, they also unknowingly brought the plague to Europe and the Middle East. Known as the Black Death, it may have killed as many as one-third of the population in the Middle East.[33] The combination of the Mongol invasions and the plague left the Muslim world seriously weakened.

29. Cavendish, "Mongols."
30. World History Edu, "What Was the Fatimid Caliphate?"
31. Hemmings, "Egyptian Mamluks."
32. Ahmed, "Ghazan the Great."
33. The plague began in China and reached Crimea by 1347 CE, spreading over the following years to most Islamic areas. Cartwright, "Black Death."

The Future of God—Part 1

Beginning in the nineteenth century, the European "Great Powers" took control of the Muslim world. Led primarily by England and France, it was carved up into nation-states. Despite the efforts of Muslim countries to build modern nation-states throughout the twentieth century, strife continues to the present day between Sunni and Shia factions. Currently, there are ongoing internal conflicts in Lebanon, Yemen, Iraq, Syria, and Pakistan.[34]

Towards the end of the twentieth century, fundamentalist factions of Islam began to resist the rapid modernization in the world, particularly from the West. When the United States led a coalition of nations to reverse the Iraqi invasion of Kuwait in 1990, it stationed some of its armed forces in Saudi Arabia. This aggravated Muslim extremists, including Osama bin Laden. Osama founded the terrorist group Al-Qaeda, which subsequently led major suicide attacks against the World Trade Center in New York City and the Pentagon in Washington, DC, on September 11, 2001. In response, the United States led a coalition of nations in an invasion of Afghanistan, where the governing Taliban group was hosting Osama bin Laden and Al-Qaeda. The attacking coalition was successful, and the United States and some of its allies remained in Afghanistan for the next two decades.

Islamic Fundamentalism

Ijtihad is a process of reform within Islam as adjudicated by an expert in Islamic law. It evolved to accommodate the changing needs of Islamic societies and advances in knowledge. The process is based on the Qur'an, religious tradition, reason, and deduction. However, toward the end of the twentieth century,

---

34. Partner, *God of Battles*, 255; McMahon, "Sunni-Shia Divide."

Islam

Islam took a turn away from ijtihad and toward fundamentalism—a reaction to Western modernization.[35]

Islamic fundamentalism is a revivalist movement that aims to return Islam to its founding scriptures: the Qur'an, Hadith, and Sunnah. They believe these scriptures should be interpreted literally, as they were intended during the time of the Prophet Muhammad. Fundamentalists reject modernization championed by the West, as well as Western secularism. They wanted non-Islamic influences to be purged from all aspects of Muslim life. Islamic fundamentalism is the driving force today in Islam, leaving little room for any changes in religious doctrine. The extreme and often selective interpretation of original Islamic sacred texts is the latest evolution of Islam.[36]

Shia Muslims award the title *mutahid* to very few of their highest-ranking clerics. And, to the highest of the *mutahid* is awarded the title of *ayatollah*. For example, the leader of the Islamic Republic of Iran is Ayatollah Sayyid Ali Khamenei. Much like Osama bin Laden, Khamenei issues guidance for all Iranians and Shia Muslims that tends to be fairly fundamentalist (i.e., anti-modernization, anti-West).[37]

---

35. Armstrong declared, "Every single one of the 'fundamentalisms' that I have studied in Judaism, Christianity, and Islam is rooted in a profound fear of annihilation, convinced that modern society wants to wipe out true faith." Armstrong, *Role of Religion*, 2. See also Khosa, "Ijtihad."
36. Easy Sociology, "Islamic Fundamentalism."
37. See Khalaji, "Iran's Anti-Western 'Blueprint.'"

Christianity

THE HISTORY OF CHRISTIANITY begins with the birth of Jesus in the beginning of the first century. It is founded on the ministry of Jesus, a Jewish preacher, teacher, and healer who was crucified around 30 CE in Jerusalem. The historical Jesus was nonviolent and rejected violent images of God that are common in the Hebrew Bible.[1]

However, the person most responsible for the origin of Christianity as a new religion was Paul the apostle. Paul, also known as Saul of Tarsus, originally persecuted early Jewish Christians. However, after a divine meeting with the resurrected Jesus on his way to Damascus, Paul was converted and baptized. He then began a mission to convert Jews and gentiles to Christianity.[2]

Paul's message to Jews and gentiles was that Jesus was the Messiah, the Son of God,[3] and that faith in him was sufficient for salvation. From the mid-thirties to the mid-fifties CE, Paul founded several Christian communities in Asia Minor and

---

1. Nelson-Pallmeyer, *Is Religion Killing Us?*, 59.
2. "As he neared Damascus on his journey, suddenly a light from heaven flashed around him. He fell to the ground and heard a voice say to him, 'Saul, Saul, why do you persecute me?' 'Who are you, Lord?' Saul asked. 'I am Jesus, whom you are persecuting,' he replied. 'Now get up and go into the city, and you will be told what you must do'" (Acts 9:3–6).
3. "And who through the Spirit of holiness was appointed the Son of God in power by his resurrection from the dead: Jesus Christ our Lord" (Rom 1:4).

Europe. Because he included gentiles, Christianity changed its character and gradually grew apart from Judaism during the first two centuries of the Christian era. Thirteen of the twenty-seven books in the New Testament have been attributed to Paul.[4]

By the fourth century, the Latin Church was unanimous about the canonical texts to be included in the New Testament. By the fifth century, the Eastern churches, with a few exceptions, had come to accept the book of Revelation as a canonical text and thus came into harmony with the Latin Church on the biblical canon.[5]

According to Aslan, the early church wanted to adopt one god because it would facilitate one bishop (later, to be the pope)—"One God, One Bishop."[6] People were told that the pope was their earthly mediator for Jesus and that no one could approach God or Jesus except through him. As such, he was to be implicitly obeyed.[7]

In 313 CE, the Roman Emperor Constantine I issued the Edict of Milan, making Christianity legal throughout the Roman Empire. He also promoted a related motto—"One God, One Emperor"—to enhance his legitimacy among Christians.[8] In 380 CE, with the Edict of Thessalonica issued by Emperor Theodosius I, the Roman Empire officially adopted Christianity as its state religion.[9] Various debates about the human versus divine nature of Jesus, the primacy of the bishop of Rome, the Virgin Mary, and other religious issues consumed the early Christian church for three centuries. As such, seven ecumenical councils were convened to resolve the various disagreements.

---

4. Sanders, "St. Paul."
5. Ackroyd and Evans, *Beginnings to Jerome*, 305.
6. Aslan, *God*, 140.
7. Wright, "Era of Spiritual Darkness."
8. Aslan, *God*, 142.
9. World History Edu, "Edict of Thessalonica."

The Future of God—Part 1

An ecumenical council is a congregation of bishops, theologians, and other church leaders who determined which divergent church policies would be followed and which would not. The councils considered Christian doctrine, governance, discipline, and other religious matters when deliberating. The primary purpose of each council was to ensure Catholicism was unified in its doctrine and teaching. Any major doctrine or policy discrepancies that had evolved since the previous council were addressed, debated, and voted on. The results of these councils were disseminated as decrees referred to as "canons." Canons have the penalty of excommunication for those who refuse to follow them.[10] The doctrine of the infallibility of ecumenical councils states that policies made by such councils (to which the whole Church must adhere) are unerring.[11] The original seven ecumenical councils were called by a Roman emperor and convened in the Eastern Roman Empire.[12]

One must remember that the church and councils consist of religious men, most of whom have competing agendas. According to Pastor Robert Evely,

> The most common teachings within the Orthodox Church today are based largely on traditions and teachings passed along through the church since the fifth century. These teachings are not based upon the word of God but upon the fallible traditions of men and the fallible translations of Scripture, which are confused and strongly influenced by the biases of the Orthodox Church.[13]

---

10. Jesus Everyday, "What Is 'Ecumenical Council.'"

11. Protestant churches generally view ecumenical councils as fallible human institutions, though they still evaluate all their pronouncements. Senz, "Authority of Ecumenical Councils."

12. 4 Marks of the Church, "Early Church Councils."

13. Evely, *End of Ages*, 89.

Christianity

There have been twenty-one ecumenical councils recognized by the Catholic Church.[14] The First Council of Nicaea in 325 CE and the First Council of Constantinople in 381 CE produced the Nicene Creed and its Trinitarian doctrine (consisting of the Father, Son, and Holy Spirit). The Council of Ephesus was convened in 431 CE by Emperor Theodosius II to reach a consensus regarding the original Nicene Creed[15] and to reject the teachings of Nestorius, the patriarch of Constantinople.[16]

By 312 CE, Christians made up approximately 10 percent of the population of the Roman Empire.[17] In the Early Middle Ages, missionary activities spread Christianity among Germans, Armenians, Georgians, Syrians, Egyptians, and Ethiopians. Christianity was essential in the development of Western civilization from around 250 to 1400 CE. With the European colonization of the Americas and other continents, Christianity expanded throughout the world.[18]

During the eleventh century, Eastern (Greek) and Western (Latin) Christianity grew apart, leading to the East-West Schism of 1054 CE. This schism was primarily a disagreement over the nature of papal primacy and the interpretation of the Nicene Creed. Still, it intensified due to cultural, geographical, geopolitical, and linguistic differences between the Greek and Latin churches. The separation became permanent with Western Christians conquering Constantinople in 1204 during the Fourth Crusade.[19]

---

14. Catholic Bridge, "21 Ecumenical Councils."

15. A creed is a doctrinal statement of religious beliefs. The Nicene Creed regards Jesus as the Son of God.

16. Catholic Bridge, "21 Ecumenical Councils." Nestorius held that the Virgin Mary should be called the "Christ-bearer" but not the "God-bearer."

17. History of Christian Theology, "Christianity."

18. New World Encyclopedia, "European Colonization."

19. New World Encyclopedia, "Great Schism."

The Future of God—Part 1

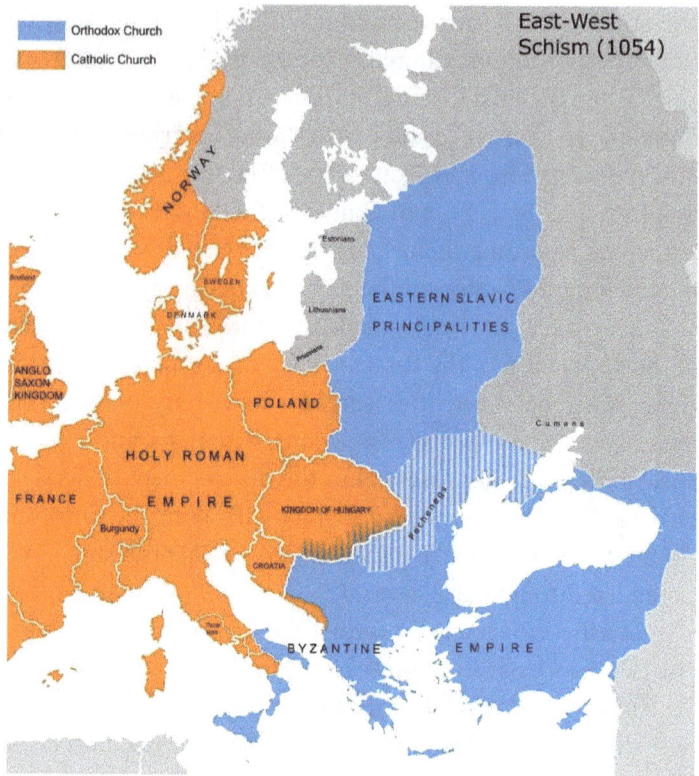

Figure 5: The Great Schism[20]

One of the primary causes of the Great Schism was the justification for and legitimacy of the Crusades. Generally, the Crusades (1095–1291 CE) were originally European Christian military campaigns sponsored by the papacy to reconquer the Holy Land in the Levant region from Muslim control. There were other Crusader expeditions against the Islamic forces in the Mediterranean, primarily in Spain, Italy, and the islands of Cyprus, Malta, and Sicily. The papacy also sponsored Crusades against: (1) the pagan peoples of Northeastern Europe (to subjugate and forcibly convert them to Christianity), (2) its

---

20. "Great Schism 1054 with Former Borders" by Tobi85, public domain, Wikimedia Commons.

political enemies in Western Europe, and (3) heretical religious minorities within Europe. With these Crusades, Christianity was proselytized by force more than by persuasion. As such, Christianity came to resemble Islam in that the sword often preceded the word of God.[21]

Figure 6: List of Crusades[22]

- First Crusade 1096–1099
- Second Crusade 1147–149
- Third Crusade 1187–1192
- Fourth Crusade 1202–1204
- Fifth Crusade 1217–1221
- Sixth Crusade 1228–1229
- Seventh Crusade 1248–1254
- Eighth Crusade 1270
- Ninth Crusade 1271–1272

Growing criticism of the Roman Catholic Church, its support for holy wars and the Crusades, and its general corruption led to the Protestant Reformation during the fifteenth and sixteenth centuries.[23] In the early sixteenth century, Christian theologians Martin Luther, John Wycliffe, Jan Hus, and Ulrich Zwingli, along with many others, attempted to reform the Catholic Church. They objected to the corruption within the Catholic Church and the notion that salvation had to be earned.[24]

The Protestant Reformation started with the publication of the *Ninety-Five Theses* by Martin Luther in 1517 CE. However, no formal schism began until the 1521 CE Diet of Worms edicts.

21. Latham, "Crusades."
22. History Lists, "List of 9 Crusades."
23. Partner, *God of Battles*, 188.
24. Weidenkopf, "Protestants."

The Future of God—Part 1

The edicts condemned Luther. For his part, Luther claimed that Pope Leo X was the antichrist and that the Crusades needed to be rejected.[25] The Protestants eventually defeated the Catholics in the Thirty Years' War (1618–1648 CE), resulting in as many as twelve million deaths throughout Europe.[26]

Once Protestantism became an established branch of Christianity, it did not take long for it to splinter. For example, fundamentalist Christianity is a movement that arose primarily within British and American Protestantism in the late nineteenth century and early twentieth century in reaction to modernism and theological liberalism. It evolved in reaction to liberal Protestant groups that denied doctrines considered fundamental to Christianity. Thus, fundamentalism sought to reestablish tenets that made up the foundation of Christianity. These fundamentals included the inerrancy of the Bible, the virgin birth of Jesus, the divinity of Jesus, the bodily resurrection of Jesus, and the second coming of Jesus Christ.[27]

Today, there are more than two billion Christians worldwide, and the number is growing. As such, Christianity, which includes Catholics, Protestants, the various branches of Protestantism, and others,[28] remains the world's largest religion. Christianity remains the predominant religion in Europe (including Russia) and the Americas (reference figure 7). It has grown rapidly in Latin America, Asia, South Korea, and much of sub-Saharan Africa.[29] Unlike most religions today, Christianity, and specifically Catholicism, continues to evolve with guidance from the resident pope to all Catholics around the world.

---

25. Partner, *God of Battles*, 189.
26. Seaver, "Thirty Years' War."
27. Pietz, "What Is Christian Fundamentalism?"
28. For example, the Church of Jesus Christ of Latter-day Saints (i.e., Mormonism).
29. Norton, "Where Is Christianity."

Christianity

Mechanisms for Change

Of the three Abrahamic religions, Christianity has the capability to evolve and adapt more easily. In Judaism and Islam, the trend has been primarily toward fundamentalism—a regression, not movement toward the future. However, Catholicism is better positioned within Christianity to accommodate future change via its many established mechanisms. Such mechanisms that can change church doctrine, beliefs, or policy include ecumenical councils, papal bulls, and other papal doctrines—all of which establish canon law.

Ecumenical Councils

As previously discussed, an ecumenical council is a meeting of bishops and church authorities to deliberate on questions of Catholic doctrine and other religious matters. Of the twenty-one recognized ecumenical councils, the first fifteen councils lasted for several months. Subsequent councils lasted for years. Each council was presided over by the presiding pope and an emperor or king to provide legitimacy. Each council consisted of at least one hundred participants, up to as many as 2,860 (the amount for Vatican II).[30]

The last two ecumenical councils convened in the Vatican are known simply as the Vatican Councils. Pope John XXIII stated that the Vatican Council's purpose was to modernize the Catholic Church after twenty centuries. The updating of the Church's traditions is commonly called *aggiornamento* ("bringing up to date," in Italian).[31]

---

30. Catholic Bridge, "21 Ecumenical Councils."
31. Senz, "Authority of Ecumenical Councils"; Carroll College, "Vatican II."

The Future of God—Part 1

Papal Bulls

A papal bull is an official document issued by a pope. Popes have been using papal bulls since the sixth century. Since the thirteenth century, popes have used papal bulls only for formal occasions. Today, a papal bull is the most formal public decree. Almost any subject may be treated in a papal bull.[32]

Encyclicals

An encyclical was originally a letter that bishops and other church authorities sent to the Roman Catholic churches in a particular area. The term is now used almost exclusively for letters disseminated by the pope to patriarchs, archbishops, and bishops to clarify church teachings or to offer insights on matters of faith and doctrine. Pope Pius XII held that papal encyclicals could be authoritative enough to end theological debate on a religious issue, thus precluding the need for another ecumenical council. As such, they are more formal than papal bulls. Pope Benedict XIV's encyclical of 1740 titled *Ubi Primum* (regarding the Immaculate Conception of Mary) is generally regarded as the first papal encyclical. There have been almost three hundred papal encyclicals issued since then. More recently, Pope Paul VI published an encyclical titled *Humanae Vitae* on the topic of birth control.[33]

Papal Documents

Recently, the presiding pope has promulgated major changes to Catholic doctrine simply by issuing a papal document from the Vatican's doctrine office. For example, on December 18, 2023, Pope Francis issued a new document that officially allowed

---

32. Messier, "Hear Ye."

33. Jesus Everyday, "What Is 'Ecumenical Council'"; Catholic Arena, "10 Papal Encyclicals"; Paul VI, *Humanae Vitae*.

priests to bless same-sex couples but not same-sex marriage (as of now). This is in line with his efforts to expand the appeal of the Catholic Church to include more people, notably from the LGBTQ community.[34]

In Practice

In general, the Catholic Church in America has become far more fragmented and less cohesive since the mid-twentieth century. Patricia Killen, a professor of humanities at Pacific Lutheran University, wrote,

> The mid-twentieth-century Roman Catholic Church was a highly cohesive community forged as an ethnic/class/religious subculture. Today, it is thoroughly assimilated into its American context; clergy and laity alike exemplify the sensibilities of this voluntary, individualistic, market and media-saturated milieu. Then, most American Catholics shared an understanding of the church as a supernatural institution, protected from the vagaries of history, and existing to mediate and dispense the means of salvation. Today, Catholics make their journey of faith through "the politics of history." The scandals over fiscal malfeasance as well as clergy sexual abuse have eroded trust among large numbers of current and former Catholics, undercutting the credibility and authority of the hierarchy. Far fewer Catholics now view the church as essential to salvation.[35]

The Second Vatican Council issued sixteen documents, such as the *Sacrosanctum Concilium* and the *Constitution on the Sacred Liturgy*, which implemented policy changes in the church. These directives advocated that the Catholic Church become more connected to its followers. These reforms focused

---

34. Sullivan, "Pope Francis." See Francis, *Fiducia Supplicans*.
35. Killen and Silk, *Future of Catholicism*, 2.

on congregations (including having the priests face the people during Mass) and on individuals.[36]

Other Christian Churches

Most of the other Christian denominations (besides Catholicism) also have mechanisms in place to change religious doctrine.[37] However, the key difference is that when the other denominations (mostly offshoots of Protestantism) make changes, the subordinate churches are generally *not* required to follow them. This is not the case within Catholicism where the pope's proclamations regarding religious doctrine are to be perceived as the word of God.

The evangelical church is a diverse group of denominations and independent churches, each with its own governance structure. Changes to fundamental doctrine require significant biblical support and the approval of two national conferences. However, differences in interpretation of Scripture can lead to variations in doctrine among different evangelical groups.[38]

The Southern Baptist Convention (SBC) has a formal mechanism for changing its fundamental doctrine, which is outlined in its constitution and bylaws. This process involves a majority vote of the executive committee at two consecutive annual conventions of the SBC. However, it's important to note that the SBC is a *cooperative* Baptist organization, meaning that individual churches maintain autonomy and are not bound to it. They are free to interpret and apply any doctrinal changes as they see fit.[39]

36. Ostberg, "Second Vatican Council."
37. Unlike Catholics, the Church of Jesus Christ of Latter-day Saints (LDS) believes in ongoing public revelation. Members believe there are still prophets who are revealing new insights from God. Conveniently, they often change their church's teachings to match the political and cultural movements of the day. Fradd, "4 Times Mormonism Changed."
38. Strand, "Rationale for Amending."
39. Roach, "SBC."

Christianity

The Presbyterian Church's guidelines for changing church doctrine resides in its constitution, called the *Book of Order*. The process begins with a proposal to the General Assembly. At that point, there is a review and recommendation followed by a debate and vote. If approved, the proposal is referred to the individual presbyteries for their consideration and vote. A majority vote by the presbyteries ratifies the proposed change.[40]

For the Lutheran Church, a proposal originates from a congregation, theological committee, or church leadership. After being studied by theological experts, the proposal requires a vote at a churchwide assembly or convention. Voting requirements for ratification can vary.[41]

The United Methodist Church (UMC) also has a formal mechanism for changing fundamental church doctrine. This process primarily involves the General Conference, the denomination's legislative body. A supermajority vote is typically required to make significant changes to the UMC's *Book of Discipline*, which contains its doctrinal standards.[42]

---

40. Presbyterian Church (U.S.A.), *Book of Order*.
41. Evangelical Lutheran Church in America, *Constitution*.
42. United Methodist Church, *Book of Discipline*.

The Future of God—Part 1

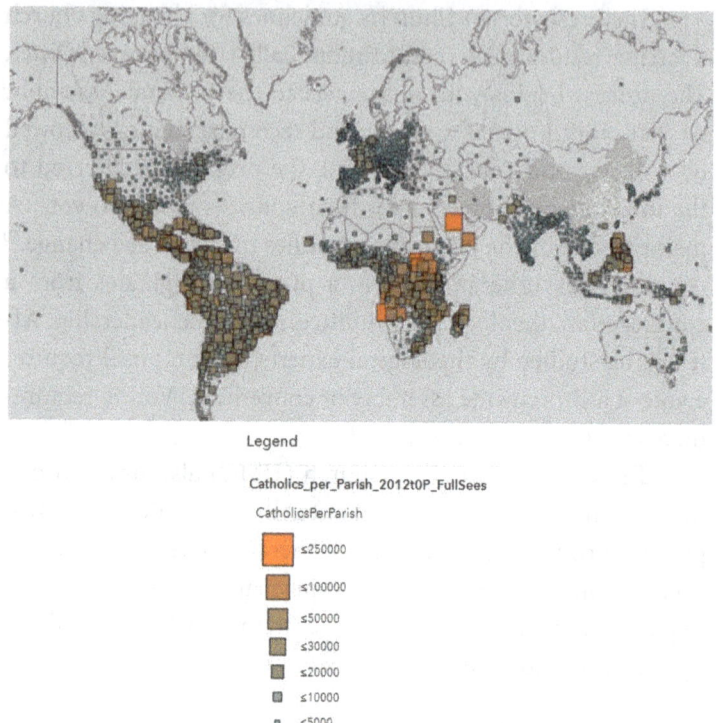

Figure 7: Map of Catholicism[43]

Religion Recap

Regarding the key question posed early on (on which of the Abrahamic religions can best determine the future of God), the answer is clearly Christianity—specifically, Catholicism. Beginning with Judaism, Jews have been fighting various elements within the Muslim world, starting with the three Israeli-Arab wars in the twentieth century. Today, Israel is at war with Iran and its proxy groups: Hamas, Houthis, and Hezbollah.

---

43. "Catholics Per Parish" courtesy of Molly Burhans, CC BY-ND 4.0 (https://creativecommons.org/licenses/by-nd/4.0/), via Catholic GeoHub (https://www.arcgis.com/home/item.html?id=64972a239c0c4782a4cb709854 8c6cc5).

Furthermore, the population of Israel is as fractured as it has ever been. While Israeli society has a long history of political division, protests against the current Netanyahu government have been ongoing for years now. A significant portion of the population is dissatisfied with the government's policies and direction. There are ongoing tensions between religious and secular Israelis along with frustration with the violence against Palestinians. Finally, there continue to be allegations against government officials of corruption. All these external and internal factors hinder any future evolution of *Yahweh*.[44]

Turning to Islam, the former empires of the Muslim world have now evolved into nation-states facilitated by European countries, as discussed previously. Unfortunately, despite the change in the nature of governance, the Sunni-Shia conflict persists both between and within today's Muslim countries. For example, the First Gulf War was an armed conflict between Shia-led Iran and Sunni-led Iraq that took place from September 1980 to August 1988. It began when Iraq invaded Iran due to Saddam Hussein's perception that Iran was weakened by its revolution in 1979. In total, around five hundred thousand people were killed. Although neither side was victorious, Iran suffered far more casualties than Iraq. The combined financial losses suffered by both countries are believed to have exceeded $1 trillion.[45]

Additionally, there are civil wars within Muslim countries, such as Iraq (since 2003), Syria (since 2011), and Yemen (since 2014), pitting Sunni and Shia factions against one another. These ongoing conflicts between Sunnis and Shias within the Muslim world have facilitated extremist fundamentalist movements that hinder any future evolution of *Allah*.[46]

---

44. *Jerusalem Post* Staff, "Jews and Arabs."

45. Iraqi Dinar US Rates News, "Iran-Iraq War."

46. It is important to note that not all conflict between and within Sunni and Shia countries are solely driven by religious differences. Political, economic, and geopolitical factors often play significant roles.

On the other hand, within the Catholic Church there has been a growing emphasis on God's love, mercy, and compassion as promoted by the Second Vatican Council (1962–1965) and the social anti-war protest and equal rights movements of the 1960s around the world. The Catholic pope continues to lead the way in reconciling God and Catholicism with societal movements worldwide through the many mechanisms available to him (as previously discussed).

Evolution of God—Theology

NOW THAT A BRIEF history of the three Abrahamic religions has been reviewed, we can see that one Abrahamic religion, more than the other two, has the capacity and will to change moving forward—Christianity. Within Christianity, Catholicism has the best capability to make major changes to Christian doctrine, such as declaring Jesus as the Son of God and Mary Magdalene as a prostitute, through ecumenical councils in the beginning and subsequently using papal decrees. Additionally, the Roman Catholic Church remains the largest religious body in the United States, with nearly sixty million people, accounting for roughly a fifth of the US population.[1]

When discussing the evolution of Christianity, there is not one approach that provides the most accurate perspective. Christopher Knight, a professor of religion at Cambridge University, found that "when studying the evolution of religion, it is also intrinsically interdisciplinary in nature."[2] In academia, several fields address the evolution of religion, including theology, sociology, biology, and physics. By analyzing the perspectives of each of these selected four fields on God, we might better determine the future of God.

---

1. Grammich, "Catholics," 1.
2. Knight, "Evolution of Religiosity," 190.

The Future of God—Part 1

Theology

To begin this section, let us define two key terms. First, theology is the systematic study of the nature of the divine. Put another way, theology is the study of God and religious faith. The study of theology guides theologians to understand religious traditions more deeply. Doug Campbell, professor of religion at the Duke University Divinity School, proposed that "theology is language that claims literally to speak accurately about God; hence, theologians sometimes refer to it usefully as 'God-talk.'"[3] God talk is what God self-revealed through the Holy Spirit and Jesus. Hence, theologians study and reflect on what God has revealed. A couple of the most famous theologians include the apostle Paul and Martin Luther.

The second definition is of God. Most theologians believe that God is omniscient, omnipresent, and omnipotent. While God is constant over time, people's perception of God is constantly changing. This changing perception of God follows human evolution and drives major changes in beliefs and church doctrine.

God and Time

One example of a change in the perception of God is God's relationship with time itself. Recently, some theologians declared that God doesn't know the future—just the past and present. As such, theology has a relatively new evolution regarding God relating to time. This evolution is called "open theism" and has been met with considerable resistance (as is the nature of most change). Many theologians still believe that God is totally in the present with the past, present, and future occurring simultaneously. W. Jay Wood, a former professor of philosophy at

---

3. Campbell, "Future," 57.

Wheaton College, claims that God is eternal and exists outside the realm of time.[4]

Conversely, Chris Mostert, a former professor of theology at the University of Divinity, believes that God is associated primarily with the future and that God's power is resident there. The future matters because the fulfillment of today's promises is a future reality.[5] Mostert claimed that human fulfillment can only manifest itself in the future.[6] Furthermore, the future can be perceived as real because it affects the present. It operates in a realm of possibilities not yet realized.[7]

For Christians, the future culminates with the kingdom of God.[8] Jesus understood the kingdom of God as being in his immediate future.[9] There could be no doubt that for Jesus the kingdom of God was a reality.[10] In fact, Jesus' resurrection can be understood as fulfilling his expectation of the imminent arrival of the kingdom of God.[11]

Open Theism

Open theism first got the attention of Christian theologians in the mid-1990s when InterVarsity Press published a symposium by five evangelical scholars under the title, *The Openness of God: A Biblical Challenge to the Traditional Understanding of God*.[12] From God's perspective, the past and future are not the same.

---

4. Wood, *God*, 192.
5. Mostert, *God*, 16.
6. Mostert, *God*, 91.
7. Mostert, *God*, 103.
8. "A nobleman [Jesus] went into a distant country to have himself appointed king and then return" (Luke 19:12).
9. Mostert, *God*, 6.
10. Mostert, *God*, 7.
11. Mostert, *God*, 53.
12. Pinnock et al., *Openness of God*, 1.

In other words, time is real for God.[13] For several people who embrace the more familiar view of God, open theism not only varies from the traditional view but also denies one of God's most fundamental qualities—being omnipresent.[14] The result is an intellectual revolution, a radical transformation regarding how evangelicals perceive God.[15]

From this new perspective of God, theological questions naturally emanate: What is the nature of time? Is time more accurately conceived as linear or progressive? And what is God's relation to time? The result is the belief of open theists that "God does not possess complete, infallible knowledge of the future."[16]

According to open theism, the world owes its existence entirely to God, and God has the power to determine the entire course of events. However, instead of doing so, God gives humankind the freedom to accept or resist God's intentions for them, and their ultimate fulfillment of his purposes requires cooperation. The reality of freedom means that God cannot achieve his purposes unilaterally.[17]

Between 1995 and 2005, numerous books appeared from evangelical publishers either defending or attacking open theism. According to Roger Olson, a professor of theology at Baylor University, many of them misrepresented open theism and dismissed open theists as non-evangelicals. Many argue that open theism denies God's sovereignty. Interestingly, almost all the critics of open theism have been Calvinists.[18]

Among the leading open theists include Gregory Boyd, an American theologian, pastor, and author; John Sanders, a professor of religious studies at Hendrix College; Clark Pinnock,

---

13. Pinnock et al., *Openness of God*, 2.
14. Pinnock et al., *Openness of God*, 3.
15. Pinnock et al., *Openness of God*, 4.
16. Pinnock et al., *Openness of God*, 82.
17. Pinnock et al., *Openness of God*, 89.
18. Brown and Silk, *Future of Evangelicalism*, 108–9. Calvinism is now a major branch of Protestantism. It began during the Protestant Reformation.

Evolution of God—Theology

a professor of theology at McMaster Divinity College; David Basinger, a professor of philosophy at Wesleyan College; and, William Hasker, a professor of philosophy at Huntington University. The open theists insisted they were not attempting to alter the doctrine of God but only to redefine "omniscience" and "omnipresence." Their view was not about God but about the nature of the future—open or closed, settled or not yet settled. They all affirmed that the end of history is settled, but not all that happens between the present and the end is settled, *so even God cannot know all that will happen.*[19] According to Richard Rice, professor emeritus of theology and philosophy of religion at Loma Linda University, past, present, and future are equally real for eternalists. But, for presentists (people who believe that things exist only in the present), "all of reality exists now, in the present; the past is no more, the future is not yet."[20]

While this new perception of God generated controversy within Evangelical American Christianity, the ideas central to open theism have endured. According to open theists, God does not know the future—perhaps including God's own.

Positivist Theology

An early threat to Christianity was the positivism movement. Positivists believe that religious belief is based in part on fear that science will overcome.[21] Knight confirmed that "religion is based primarily upon fear, . . . fear of mysterious, defeat, death. Science can help us to get over this craven fear."[22] Stark also confirmed this, stating, "Religion arises mainly out of fear. Faith is sustained by ignorance."[23] Smith also believed this but from a psychological perspective. He wrote, "Psychologists have come

19. Brown and Silk, *Future of Evangelicalism*, 108.
20. Rice, *Future of Open Theism*, 84.
21. Armstrong, *History of God*, 379.
22. Knight, "Evolution of Religiosity," 223.
23. Stark, *Discovering God*, 1.

to have serious doubts about the efficacy of fear as a deterrent to wrongdoing."[24]

Auguste Comte (1798–1857) first articulated modern positivism in the early nineteenth century. Positivism holds that all knowledge is derived from facts, reason, logic, or sensory experience. Smith defined it as "the assumption that the methods of natural science are the only approach to valid knowledge."[25] The positivist paradigm is that religion belonged to humanity's infancy. It was a necessary stage in the transition from childhood to maturity. Now that humanity has advanced technologically, religion can be left behind.[26]

One significant positivist movement during the twentieth century was the declaration that *God is dead*. Friedrich Nietzsche (1844–1900) was a German philosopher whose work profoundly influenced philosophy. He believed that God was "pitiable, absurd, and a crime against life" that should be perceived only as an illusion.[27] In line with this thinking, Armstrong observed that throughout history people have discarded their conception of God when it no longer suited them.[28] There are two explanations for this observation. First, the world's suffering throughout history led many people to conclude that God does not exist.[29] Second, advances in science and technology have created a new spirit of autonomy and independence, which has led people to declare independence from God.[30] John Caputo, a professor of philosophy at Villanova University, confirmed this perception by writing,

> Religion, with its unrelenting supernaturalism and mythologizing, is making itself more and more unbelievable

24. Smith, *Why Religion Matters*, 36.
25. Smith, *Why Religion Matters*, 84.
26. Armstrong, *History of God*, 357.
27. Armstrong, *History of God*, 356–57.
28. Armstrong, *History of God*, 356.
29. Wood, *God*, 159.
30. Armstrong, *History of God*, 346.

Evolution of God—Theology

and is seeing to it that belief flourishes best among the most deprived and desperate, the poorest and most undereducated people on the globe, while finding itself increasingly irrelevant to everyone else. We are fast approaching the point where once an individual or a culture reaches a certain stage of intellectual clarity and economic stability, even after centuries of doctrinal servitude, its religious beliefs become, well, unbelievable and incur mass incredulity.[31]

However, according to Daniel Conway, a professor of philosophy and humanities at Texas A&M University, "What the death of God does not mean is that humanity no longer enjoys any access to, or appreciation of, the divine."[32] He believes that while some perceptions of the divine have grown obsolete, that does not mean that other conceptions of the divine do not evolve to accommodate present realities.[33] Like Conway, Richard Rorty, a former professor of philosophy at Princeton University, and Gianni Vattimo, a former professor of philosophy at the University of Turin, believed that the Death of God movement was not anti-Christian but looked beyond Christianity.[34] They also believed that postmodern man would become "an agent responsible no longer to God but to himself and others."[35]

The Death of God movement peaked in the 1960s.[36] As Caputo observed, "Every time the death of God is announced, a funny thing happens on the way to the funeral. Every time religion is pronounced dead at the scene, religion revives and lives on to bury its own undertakers."[37] As such, this movement morphed into a theology known as radical theology (RT).

31. Caputo, *Folly of God*, 76.
32. Conway, "Exemplarity," 155.
33. Conway, "Exemplarity," 155.
34. Rorty and Vattimo, *Future of Religion*, 2.
35. Rorty and Vattimo, *Future of Religion*, 14.
36. Robbins, *Radical Theology*, 14.
37. Caputo, *Folly of God*, 47.

It is important to note that radical theology is a diverse movement, and not all theologians within this movement embraced its themes or ideas. Radical theology fosters dialogue with other religions and even with atheism. Its scholars explore the intersections of Christianity with Judaism, Islam, and secular humanism, emphasizing the need for open and inclusive conversations. As a movement, it encompasses constructive, secular, and political theologies.[38]

Another RT theme is process theology, or theism. This concept envisions that the universe is populated by agents of free will and self-determination. According to Donald Viney, a philosophy professor at Pittsburg State University, "Process theism does not deny that God is in some respects eternal, immutable, and impassible, but it contradicts the classical view by insisting that God is in some respects temporal, mutable, and passible."[39] This means that God does not control events, just the possibilities that can occur. This concept seeks to reconcile religious thought with modern scientific understanding.

Theodicy

Explaining how a benevolent and all-powerful God can permit suffering and evil to occur, especially among children and animals, is known as "theodicy." Theodicy is one of the primary reasons people have lost faith in God throughout history.

One popular tenet of theodicy argues that evil is a consequence of God giving humans free will. Free will is perceived as critical for humankind, even though it allows for the possibility of moral evil.[40]

Another tenet of theodicy is that God allows evil to exist because it helps in spiritual growth. Through suffering and

---

38. Grimshaw, "Radical Theologies."
39. Viney, "Process Theism," §8.
40. Camilleri, "Aquinas," §4.

hardship, human souls are strengthened and developed, making the existence of evil necessary for a higher moral and spiritual purpose. As such, evil and suffering are necessary stages in this growth, enabling humans to freely choose good to get closer to God. In other words, "no pain, no gain."[41]

However, this tenet of theodicy does not make sense if God is responsible for natural weather phenomena such as hurricanes, tornadoes, drought, floods, tsunamis, earthquakes, fire, and lightning, among others, that have caused mass human suffering throughout history.[42] Humans are not responsible for such phenomena—perhaps only for the intensity of such events over the past several decades (i.e., global warming).

A third tenet is the "greater good" defense which suggests that some evils are permitted by God because they lead to a greater good. For example, enduring hardship can develop virtues like compassion, patience, and courage, which might not appear in people if they lived in a world devoid of suffering.[43]

Future of God—Theology

This section discussed key aspects of how the field of theology perceives God and religion. One significant evolution in theology is the new perception that God does not control the future—that God is not totally in the present with the past, present, and future occurring simultaneously. Next, some theologians believe God evolves as humanity evolves. Finally, as humankind evolves, many theologians question how a benevolent god can allow so much human suffering.

The bottom line regarding the future of God from the theological perspective is that God evolves as humankind evolves. With modernization increasing, God appears to be becoming less and less essential to people's lives. As the world modernizes,

---

41. Camilleri, "Aquinas," §4.
42. Often termed "acts of God" by insurance company exclusions.
43. Camilleri, "Aquinas," §4.

The Future of God—Part 1

God is likely to be celebrated more culturally and historically in societies.

Evolution of God—Sociology

ACCORDING TO THE AMERICAN Sociological Association (ASA), sociology studies "social life, social change, and the social causes and consequences of human behavior."[1] The ASA further explains,

> Sociologists investigate the structure of groups, organizations, and societies and how people interact within these contexts. Since all human behavior is social, the subject matter of sociology ranges from the intimate family to the hostile mob; from organized crime to religious traditions; from the divisions of race, gender, and social class to the shared beliefs of a common culture.[2]

Sociologists study religion as both a belief system—how people see the world—and a social institution—an organizational structure where members are socialized. Such organizations consist of social activities organized around a religion—such as in a church. Nicholaus Nelson-Goedert, a sociology professor at Miami Dade College, noted that in any society, people are socialized by family, peers, education, media, and religion, among others.[3]

Sociologists credit Émile Durkheim as the founder of modern sociology. His book, *The Study of Suicide*, was published in

1. American Sociological Association, "What Is Sociology?"
2. American Sociological Association, "What Is Sociology?"
3. Crossman, "Sociology of Religion"; Nelson-Goedert, "Power of Socialization."

1897. In it, he explored the suicide rates among Catholics and Protestants. Durkheim concluded that religion brought people together by promoting a sense of belonging.[4] Since then, sociology has evolved into four primary perspectives: functional, economic, conflict, and social behaviorism.

Functional Perspective

Durkheim began the functional perspective of religion. Religion has been integral to society, serving to maintain social order while providing norms, values, and culture. Churches play a key role in socialization, along with family, friends, school, and the media.[5]

Economic Perspective

Following Durkheim, Max Weber and Karl Marx also looked at religion's role and influence in other fields, such as economics and politics. Max Weber, a German sociologist, philosopher, and political economist, made significant contributions regarding the role of religion in society. He argued that religious beliefs were a powerful force in shaping the values of individuals that in turn influenced the economy. He proposed that the Calvinist strict work ethic contributed to the development of a disciplined approach to work that, in turn, facilitated the growth of capitalism. While Weber acknowledged the importance of cultural and ideological factors, such as religion, Karl Marx emphasized economic factors as the primary driver of social change.[6]

---

4. Crossman, "Sociology of Religion."
5. Crossman, "Sociology of Religion."
6. Bhadauria, "Max Weber," 17–22.

Evolution of God—Sociology

Conflict Perspective

Karl Marx argued that society is divided into distinct classes based on the means of production. The ruling class owns the means of production, while the working class provides the necessary labor. Marx believed that religion was used to legitimize the existing social order and to maintain class oppression. It supported a hierarchy of people and the subordination of humankind to a divine authority. Marx focused on the roles of power, inequality, and conflict as shaping social structures. He famously remarked that religion was the opium of the people. They both make suffering more bearable.[7]

Marx's dominant ideology thesis posits that socialization is how the dominant class imposes its values and ideology on the rest of society. Socialization is used to reinforce the existing class structure and perpetuate the interests of the ruling class.[8]

Figure 8: Founders of sociology[9]

Social Behaviorism

The fourth perspective is social behaviorism, which is based on the writings of George H. Mead, a professor of sociology at the University of Chicago, and Erving Goffman, a professor of

7. Singh, "Marx on Religion."
8. Oxford Reference, "Dominant Ideology."
9. Images of Émile Durkheim and Max Weber courtesy of Tonnies, CC BY-SA 4.0 (https://creativecommons.org/licenses/by-sa/4.0/), Wikimedia Commons. Image of Karl Marx by John Jabez Edwin Paisley Mayall, public domain, Wikimedia Commons.

sociology at the University of Pennsylvania. Social behaviorism refers to the influence of the social environment on human behavior. Mead's work focused on the development of the self. He wrote that "every individual self within a given society or social community reflects in its organized structure the whole relational pattern of organized social behavior which that society or community exhibits."[10] In other words, one's mind develops from the social interaction with others. Along with social behaviorism, Mead also developed the philosophy of pragmatism.

Pragmatism is a philosophy that Mead identified using four general tenets:

- True reality does not exist but is created by how we act.
- People base their knowledge on what has been helpful to them.
- People define social and physical "objects" according to their use of them.
- We must base understanding on what people actually do.[11]

Let's examine how faith in God and religion might apply to these four general tenets. God and religion can be perceived as true reality as most people subscribe to one or both. As for changing what does not work for people, this might be reflected in the declining attendance at religious services in many places worldwide. It appears that organized religion as an institution is not working for people as it has in the past, particularly among younger adults.

As for defining social objects, we now have new definitions for religious people, particularly for those who continue to have faith but do not participate in religious services. Despite the secularization of modern societies, religion remains relevant for many people needing solace, comfort, and hope.[12]

10. Mead, *Mind, Self, and Society*, 93.
11. Mead, *Mind, Self, and Society*, 63–104.
12. Farhan, "Evolving Beliefs."

Evolution of God—Sociology

Five Social Areas

It is important to note that the sociology of religion is a dynamic field where researchers explore various aspects of religious phenomena from different perspectives. Let's consider five areas sociologists study regarding God: secularization, pluralism, reinterpretation, persistence, and Deism / nontheistic beliefs.[13]

Secularization

Secularization refers to the declining influence of religion in society. It is, in essence, the concept of separation of church and state. Stephen Jay Gould, a professor of evolutionary biology at both Harvard University and the University of New York, pioneered the concept of "non-overlapping magisteria" (NOMA). It suggests that science and religion represent distinct domains that do not overlap in their respective functions. Gould argues that these two domains are fundamentally different and should not conflict. By recognizing the distinct roles of science and religion, scholars can avoid unnecessary clashes and appreciate the unique value of each.[14]

However, some scholars have issues with NOMA despite its popularity. They argue that it is overly simplistic and does not adequately address the overlap between scientific and religious claims, particularly in areas like cosmology, biology, and ethics. Richard Dawkins, a professor of evolutionary biology at the University of Oxford, concluded that NOMA is unrealistic and that religion cannot be divorced from scientific matters.[15] Daniel Dennett, a professor of philosophy at Tufts University, argued that religion often incorporates scientific claims and

---

13. In addition to these areas, sociologists of religion have also examined topics such as religious institutions, rituals, identity, movements, and the role of religion in shaping social structures and norms.

14. Gould, *Rocks of Ages*, 5.

15. Dawkins, "When Religion Steps," 18.

that NOMA fails to address the complex interplay between the two domains.[16] Finally, Francis Collins, a geneticist and former director of the National Institutes of Health, agreed that science cannot answer ultimate questions of meaning and purpose, but that science and religion are not entirely separate.[17]

Given the trend towards less religiosity, secularization is becoming the norm in modern societies around the world. Many sociologists have argued that as societies become more secular, belief in traditional religious conceptions of God declines. They point to trends in many Western societies where religiosity and belief in God have decreased. However, it is essential to note that this is not a universal trend, as religiosity and belief in God remain strong in many parts of the third world (likely due to not being as modernized).[18]

In the United States, Americans are becoming less religious. They are leaving organized religion. Only a minority of American adults even belong to a church, synagogue, or mosque anymore. Furthermore, some forty million American adults have stopped going to church altogether. If trends continue, by the mid-2030s fewer than half of Americans will identify as Christians.[19]

Post-Secularism

Armstrong set the stage for post-secularism, observing that

> in the middle of the twentieth century, it was widely assumed that secularism was the coming ideology and that religion would never again play a major role in world events. But in almost every single one of the major world religions—in Judaism, Christianity, Islam, Hinduism, Sikhism, Buddhism, and Confucianism—an aggressive

16. Hameed, "Dennett."
17. Mello-Klein, "Science and Religion."
18. Sociology Institute, "Process of Secularization."
19. Kristof, "America."

piety, that is deeply political, has challenged this assumption, determined to drag God/religion from the sidelines to which they have been relegated in modern secular society and back to center stage. In almost every region where a secularized society, separating religion and politics, has been established a religious counter-cultural movement has sprung up alongside it in conscious rejection, displaying a widespread disappointment with modernity.[20]

Post-secularism suggests that rather than a decline in religion, societies may move beyond a separation of the secular and religious realms. In a post-secular world, religious and secular perspectives may coexist and influence each other more openly. Muhammad Golam Nabi Mozumder, a professor of sociology at the University of Pittsburg, proposed post-secularism to address "the continued existence of religious communities in a continually secularizing environment."[21] Habermas suggested that religion and the secular must learn from each other, not subordinate one to the other.[22]

Linear Evolution of Secularism

Credit for coining the term "sociology" is usually given to the French philosopher Auguste Comte. Comte believed in a linear evolution of secularization. He thought that it evolved in three consecutive stages. In the first stage (theological), humanity looked to the gods and deities to make sense of the universe. In the second stage (metaphysical), humanity held on to intangible notions that extended the first stage. In these two stages, there was no secularization of society. In the third stage (scientific), humanity did away with faith and based societal laws on the scientific method and rationality. Comte, however, was aware

---

20. Armstrong, *Role of Religion*, 2.
21. Mozumder, "Interrogating Post-Secularism," 4.
22. Welker, "Habermas and Ratzinger," 456.

that the three stages of thinking may coexist in the same society or may not always be successive.[23]

Pluralism

Pluralism requires the active engagement of different cultural, religious, and social groups within a society. (Otherwise, it is just an example of diversity.) It is when people in a society embrace diversity and become educated about the differences that pluralism emerges. As such, growing up in a pluralistic society exposes individuals to different customs, traditions, and belief systems.[24]

With globalization and migration, various religious traditions are mixing and coexisting (known as syncretism). This can lead to a more pluralistic view of God, where people are exposed to and may adopt beliefs from multiple faiths. According to Robert Wright, a professor of philosophy at Princeton University, gods are products of cultural evolution. Hence, endless cross-fertilization of God and religion occurs over time.[25]

Today, the younger generations tend not to accept religious institutions or labels. While they may still be spiritual, they tend not to be that religious—they prefer to personalize their faith. In 2017, a quarter of Americans perceived themselves as spiritual but not religious. This is a growing trend.[26] The consequence of such individual faith is the decline in organized religion. This has manifested itself with meetings of younger Americans in coffee shops, libraries, and restaurants to discuss faith while avoiding church services and sermons.[27]

---

23. Sociology Institute, "Auguste Comte's Law."
24. Pluralism Project, "Diversity to Pluralism."
25. Wright, *Evolution of God*, 125.
26. Lloyd-Moffet, "Future of Religion."
27. Lloyd-Moffet, "Future of Religion."

Reinterpretation

Reinterpretation involves reevaluating existing beliefs and traditions in response to changes in society and advancements in science and technology. It can challenge traditional norms and encourage individuals to critically reassess their values. Heikki Räisänen, a professor of theology at the University of Helsinki, wrote that

> religious thought develops in a process in which traditions are time and again interpreted in the light of new experiences, and vice versa: experiences are interpreted in the light of traditions. In other words, elements of the tradition are reinterpreted, but this happens in the framework of the very tradition in question.[28]

Sociologists also study changes within religious institutions. They explore how traditional religious organizations adapt to societal changes, including shifts in values, demographics, and technology. Religious institutions, such as Catholicism, must evolve and adapt to remain relevant. Thomas Plante, a professor of psychology at Santa Clara University, concluded that "contemporary times and changing lifestyles associated with numerous and fast-moving cultural shifts have resulted in the evolution of our religion and spiritual engagement into more of an individualistic, personal, and private matter rather than a group or a communal one."[29]

Persistence

Persistence is the continued prevalence of certain beliefs, values, or practices over time. Persistent cultural or religious beliefs can shape the socialization process by providing a foundation for individuals, influencing their identity, and guiding their

---

28. Räisänen, "Tradition, Experience, Interpretation," 215–16.

29. Plante, "Religious and Spiritual Communities," 791. This adaptationist approach is also part of the biology field.

behavior within a particular cultural or religious framework.[30] Paola Giuliano, a professor of management at UCLA, and Nathan Nunn, a professor of economics at the University of British Columbia, conducted a study about when cultural persistence is most effective. They found that "relying on tradition is more beneficial in environments that are more stable from one generation to the next."[31] Andrew Greeley, a professor of sociology at the University of Arizona, wrote that "religion has not died. . . . The Gallup World Poll confirms that more than 90 percent of people in every country in the world believe in God."[32]

Most sociologists believe that belief in God will persist. They argue that human beings have a fundamental need for meaning and purpose in life that believing in God satisfies. Religion has been credited with soothing anxiety, and it protects people from stress and the diseases related to it.[33] Research shows that religious Americans (50 percent) are generally happier and less stressed than the nonreligious.[34] Along this line of reasoning, Kardong determined that "humans are psychologically primed for religion," which explains its persistence over many millennia.[35]

Religion may experience a resurgence in the future. Some sociologists believe societal challenges and uncertainties could lead to a renewed interest in spirituality and a return to traditional religious frameworks.[36] Over the long run, religious practices continue because they are adaptive behaviors suited to the local environment.[37]

---

30. Giuliano and Nunn, "Understanding Cultural Persistence," 1.
31. Giuliano and Nunn, "Understanding Cultural Persistence," 47.
32. Greeley, *Persistence of Religion*, 246.
33. Kardong, *Beyond God*, 123.
34. Shelby, *Evolution*, 49.
35. Kardong, *Beyond God*, 124.
36. Gobry, "Why Religion Will Dominate."
37. Kardong, *Beyond God*, 150. Religions often adapt to their environments to stay relevant. For example, within Christianity, such adaptations occurred

Evolution of God—Sociology

Deism / Nontheistic Beliefs

Deism is the belief in a higher power or creator (often without adherence to specific religious doctrines). In contrast, nontheistic beliefs encompass various worldviews that do not involve a personal deity. However, growing up with either deistic or nontheistic beliefs is more likely to lead to a more secular worldview. Deism posits a distant, non-intervening creator God while nontheistic belief systems (such as Buddhism) emphasize the pursuit of spiritual enlightenment without a divine deity.[38]

To complete this chapter on the future of God according to sociology, we should discuss two fields of study that may have an impact: the cognitive science of religion and the adaptationist approach.

Cognitive Science of Religion

The cognitive science of religion (CSR) is the application of cognitive capacities to determine how people acquire and transmit the traditions of religion. Its focus is on the origin of religious beliefs. One reason for studying CSR is to determine the commonalities of religion across world societies. Cognitive capacities consist of the information gathered from one's basic senses (i.e., sight, hearing, smell, taste, and touch) that enable people to function in their environment. Examples of cognitive capacities related to information processing include memory, decision-making, problem-solving, and planning.[39]

The study of religion as a cognitive phenomenon began with the cognitive revolution of the 1960s.[40] Per-Johan Norelius,

---

in the early twentieth century with the Pentecostal movement and Christian fundamentalism, and again in the mid-twentieth century with the civil rights movement and Progressive Christianity.

38. This vs. That, "Deism vs. Theism."
39. NeuronUp, "Cognitive Abilities."
40. Miller, "Cognitive Revolution," 141.

a professor of theology at Uppsala University, summarized CSR as follows:

> The so-called cognitive study of religion arose in the 1980s and 1990s as an attempt to bring methods from the "hard" sciences into religious studies, including the use of experiments and other ways of advancing testable hypotheses. It draws on the cognitive sciences as well as evolutionary psychology, which means that it concerns itself with biological evolution proper and seeks answers to the existence of religious beliefs in the remote prehistory of mankind. Humans are held to have an innate tendency towards beliefs in spirits, deities, souls, and afterlife, due to intuitions developed throughout a long history of evolution. The cognitive study of religion—whose adherents hail from a variety of backgrounds: religious studies, anthropology, psychology, philosophy, and the natural sciences—is a comparatively young subdiscipline of religious studies and by no means an uncontroversial one.[41]

As an example of the controversy surrounding CSR, Taede Smedes, a professor of theology at the Catholic university in Leuven (KU Leuven), Belgium, assessed it as follows: "I hold that the CSR cannot and does not say anything about God, but is all about belief in God."[42]

Adaptationist Approach to Religion

The adaptationist approach to religion seeks to understand the function of religion using evolutionary principles. This approach suggests that religion evolved because it conferred adaptive advantages regarding survival and reproduction. The adaptationist perspective is that religion evolved because it provided benefits for group cohesion, cooperation, and social bonding among early human communities. Religious traditions

---

41. Norelius, "Origins of Soul-Beliefs," 38.
42. Evers et al., *Is Religion Natural?*, 186.

Evolution of God—Sociology

may have promoted cooperation and trust among group members, enhancing their chances of survival and reproduction. According to Konrad Szocik, a professor of philosophy at Yale University, "religious beliefs increase the chances of survival and reproduction of the whole group that shares them."[43]

While the adaptationist approach provides valuable insights into the origins of religion, it has also faced criticism. Critics have argued that reducing religion solely to adaptive functions overlooks cultural and environmental factors. Szocik provided a keen bottom-line insight stating that "both cognitive and adaptationist approaches are highly speculative."[44]

The cognitive and adaptationist approaches regarding religion have more applicability to how humanity became religious in the beginning. Today, these approaches may have more applicability in explaining why humankind is *moving away* from being religious. Both the evolutionary cognition and the adaptationist approach can be applied to post-industrial revolution societies to identify how people, societies, and cultures change with the advances of science. For example, religious people tend to have higher fertility rates than secularized people. But, in today's modern society, high reproduction rates are often correlated with high crime rates and general societal problems.[45] As such, the trend is moving more toward secular societies.

CSR and the adaptationist approach can help explain the decline in religious faith worldwide. During human evolution, scientific discoveries explained much of what was once believed to be of the realm of God. Cognition is also responsible for people wondering how so much evil can exist in the world when, allegedly, there is a benevolent God. The adaptationist approach sees religions around the world with either no God or millions of gods. There are only a few established religions that are monotheistic. In the era of instant gratification and

43. Szocik, "Religion," 36.
44. Szocik, "Critical Remarks," 162.
45. Szocik, "Religion," 39.

twenty-four seven connectivity, the timeless nature of religious rituals is being overcome. Busy schedules mean less time for religious reflection and community gatherings. Many people in modern societies, such as the United States, find that there is little to no room left for religion in their lives in today's world.

Miracles

In today's societies around the world, one may wonder why there are no more miracles, prophets, or divine human beings? (The last prophet was the Prophet Muhammad in the seventh century, and the last miracle in the Bible was Jesus restoring the severed ear of the high priests' servant, Malchus.[46]) According to Deepak Chopra, a professor of medicine at Tufts University, Boston University, and Harvard University, "The age of miracles seems to lie somewhere in the past."[47] Belief in miracles persisted during the Roman Empire. In the first century BCE, Apollonius of Tyana was believed to produce miracles like Jesus, including raising people from the dead.[48]

Dawkins claimed that true miracles could never have existed simply because they violate the principles of science.[49] Augustine of Hippo (354–430 CE) defined a miracle as "whatever appears that is arduous or unusual beyond the hope and power of them who wonder."[50] He believed that miracles do not differ essentially from natural events; however, they attract more human attention because they are beyond man's expectations. We see examples of "miracles" today, primarily through a

---

46. "And one of them struck the servant of the high priest, cutting off his right ear. But Jesus answered, 'No more of this!' And he touched the man's ear and healed him" (Luke 22:50–51).
47. Chopra, *Future of God*, 127.
48. Kokkinidis, "Ancient Greek Jesus Christ."
49. Dawkins, *God Delusion*, 83.
50. Harden, "Concept of Miracle," 230.

Evolution of God—Sociology

remarkable performance by an individual or team in a sporting event.[51]

Faith and Education

Related to this, Phil Zuckerman, a professor of sociology at Pitzer College, determined that there is a negative correlation between religiosity and education (i.e., the more educated people are, the less likely they are to be religious).[52] It turns out that the world is becoming more and more educated every year. The United Nations Educational, Scientific, and Cultural Organization reported that there have been increases in all levels of education during the last half of the twentieth century.[53] At the same time, adult illiteracy rates have decreased significantly. Within the past century, the number of children worldwide enrolled in school has increased by over a third.[54]

Related to higher education is computer digital literacy. The digital generations (those people who grew up using computers) are known for challenging the status quo. With information at their fingertips, they are more informed and less likely to accept things at face value, including religious beliefs.[55]

In today's world, seeing is believing. The call for concrete evidence leaves many people uncertain about religion. Little evidence outside of the Bible proves that it is true.[56] The same

---

51. The "Miracle on Ice" was a hockey game played during the Winter Olympics in Lake Placid, New York. The game was played on February 22, 1980, and featured amateur players from the United States against professional players from the Soviet Union. The American amateur team defeated the Soviet professional team—hence the reference.

52. Zuckerman, "Education Corrodes Religious Faith."

53. Matsuura, "Ending Poverty."

54. Galan, "Number of Pupils."

55. Wittberg, "Generational Change."

56. Lemonick, "Bible's Stories."

is true for the existence of Jesus or Moses.[57] Some folks struggle with the concept of faith, relying instead on hard evidence to form their beliefs. Many people today tend to pick and choose which aspects of their religion to believe in when it suits them. The idea that one can pick and choose what to believe about what God said implies that none of it really matters.

A syndicated columnist, Nicholas Kristof authored a perspective of America losing faith in 2003. In it, he stated that the industrialized world has become more secular, and there is evidence that Americans are becoming significantly less religious.[58] Opinion poll results substantiated this declining shift in faith. Twenty years later, in 2023, a Gallup poll found that people who felt religion was "very important" in their lives dropped from 61 percent to 45 percent.[59] Additionally, forty million Americans have stopped attending church in the past twenty-five years, representing the largest drop in American history.[60] In 2023, only 20 percent of Americans attended church once a week (on Sundays), down from 32 percent in 2000.[61]

For decades, mainline Protestant denominations have been losing members while conservative evangelical traditions have at least maintained their members. Between 2000 and 2015, Protestant evangelical churches experienced a slight increase in their membership while the Presbyterian Church, Episcopal Church, and United Church of Christ each lost 40

---

57. Lataster, "Historical Jesus"; Flem-Ath, "Moses."
58. Kristof, "America."
59. Gallup, "Religion."
60. Meador, "Misunderstood Reason." It should be noted that there are reports that while religious disaffiliation may be growing in America, it may be the opposite for the rest of the world. However, in one 2016 report on the Internet by Pascal Gobry, a former fellow at the Ethics and Public Policy Center, he cited many countries where religion appeared to be gaining strength. However, in each case, he did not mention that the number of religious people in those countries was less than half the total population. Gobry, "Why Religion Will Dominate."
61. ChurchTrac, "State of Church Attendance."

percent of their membership. In contrast, Protestant evangelical churches saw a slight increase in membership—but only during the first decade of this century.[62]

However, today that is no longer the case. Reporting of church attendance by denominations and traditions of all beliefs shows the lowest attendance rates ever seen in America's history, including the conservative evangelical churches. In an article in the *Religion News Service* in July 2023, Robert Smietana reported that "the twenty-first century has been hard on God" and that "losing faith in God seems to be accompanied by disbelief in the devil."[63] A poll of 1,011 adult Americans taken in May 2023 showed that belief in God dropped from 90 percent in 2001 to 74 percent in 2023. Belief in heaven was down from 83 percent to 67 percent, while belief in angels dropped from 79 percent to 69 percent. In fact, some scholars believe God will become extinct during the twenty-first century.[64]

This shift in faith includes the changing of religions as well. According to a recent survey of religious affiliation by the Pew Forum, more than a quarter of adult Americans changed their original religious faith to join another religion or adopt no religion at all. It appears that 44 percent of all Americans have switched religious affiliations.[65] In 2008, Neela Banerjee, a syndicated journalist, reported in the *New York Times* that "for at least a generation, scholars have noted that more Americans are moving among faiths, as denominational loyalty erodes."[66]

While 81 percent of Americans still believe in God,[67] most Americans disagree on who God is or how God relates to their personal lives. Representing many philosophers, Caputo

---

62. ChurchTrac, "State of Church Attendance."
63. Smietana, "Organized Religion."
64. Smietana, "Organized Religion."
65. Banerjee, "Fluid Religious Life."
66. Banerjee, "Fluid Religious Life."
67. Gallup, "How Many Americans Believe." This percentage is down from 87 percent in 2017.

believes God and his kingdom are *within* each of us.[68] When people say, "I'm spiritual, but I'm not religious," they usually mean that they value a private connection with the divine, but they have no interest in religious organizations.[69] Connecting with other church members no longer plays a vital role in one's spiritual life, and participating with others in worship is reduced to a matter of personal preference.[70] As such, people are responsible for their actions and should not justify them using God or religion.[71]

Finally, Armstrong observed that a God who tinkered with the universe was absurd, and a God who interfered with human freedom was a tyrant.[72] She concluded that when religious beliefs lose their validity, they usually fade away. She wrote, "If the human idea of God no longer works . . . it will be discarded."[73]

The bottom line is that evidence is growing that Americans are becoming significantly less religious. They are drifting away from religion and churches and are less likely to say religion is important in their lives going forward.

Future of God—Sociology

Sociologists, like academics in other disciplines, have diverse perspectives on the future of God and religion. It is essential to note that sociology itself does not make predictions about spiritual matters but rather observes and analyzes social phenomena. Individual beliefs and practices can vary widely, making it challenging to predict a singular trajectory for the future of God from a sociological standpoint.

---

68. Caputo, *Folly of God*, 114.
69. Caputo, *Folly of God*, 207.
70. Caputo, *Folly of God*, 209.
71. Rorty and Vattimo, *Future of Religion*, 14.
72. Armstrong, *History of God*, 382.
73. Armstrong, *History of God*, 397.

Evolution of God—Sociology

Kardong determined that humans are predisposed psychologically toward religion.[74] Early on, God and religion were used to overcome environmental challenges for humanity to survive.[75] Along with various academics, he found that religion was not exempt from evolutionary processes.[76] As humans evolved to become more scientific, they have needed religion and God less and less.

Wright believed that two positions dominate discussion of the virtues of religion: (1) people who think religion serves society broadly (providing reassurance and hope) and brings social cohesion, and (2) people who think religion is a tool for social control. Perhaps neither position is accurate today.[77] Certainly, social order today can be maintained without the power of religion. Instead of religion being used to control society, it seems to be threatening the global social system with chaos.

As such, the general trend in sociology supports secularism over religious persistence. Societies around the world are modernizing, which in turn has seen the downsizing of religion in many regards (e.g., the lowering of regular attendance at church services) and of the belief in God.

---

74. Kardong, *Beyond God*, 124.
75. Kardong, *Beyond God*, 272.
76. Kardong, *Beyond God*, 28.
77. Wright, *Evolution of God*, 25, 44.

Evolution of God—Biology

IN GENERAL TERMS, BIOLOGY is the scientific study of life. Specifically, biologists study life's mechanisms, evolution processes, genetics, ecology, and other aspects of organisms. It is considered a hard science compared to sociology, which is regarded as a soft science.

According to Stark, to search for a biological basis for faith is "a misguided waste of time."[1] Despite that, he noted that questions about God are now dominated by biologists and evolutionary psychologists.[2] However, very few biologists have published research on the viability of God.

---

1. Stark, *Discovering God*, 43.
2. Stark, *Discovering God*, 1.

Evolution of God—Biology

Figure 9: Richard Dawkins[3]

Richard Dawkins, a prominent evolutionary biologist, is widely known for being an atheist and criticizing religion, particularly in his book *The God Delusion*. In it and in various public appearances, Dawkins discussed the origins of religion and explored sociological explanations for why humans are prone to religious beliefs.[4]

From Dawkins's perspective, there is no empirical evidence or scientific proof for the existence of God. There are several reasons why Dawkins does not believe in God, including evolutionary biology, the problem of evil, the critique of religious beliefs, Occam's Razor, and cultural and psychological factors.

Dawkins' work in evolutionary biology has led him to view the world through the lens of natural selection and evolution (see Darwin). He considers the complexity of life as a product of natural processes without the need for divine intervention.[5]

---

3. "Richard Dawkins Cooper Union Shankbone" courtesy of David Shankbone, CC BY 3.0 (https://creativecommons.org/licenses/by/3.0/), Wikimedia Commons.

4. Dawkins, *God Delusion*, 248–49. See "Cognitive Science of Religion" in the previous section.

5. Dawkins, *God Delusion*, 190.

Like many other atheists, Dawkins grapples with the religious problem of evil, which questions how an all-powerful, all-knowing, and benevolent God could allow suffering to exist in the world. The presence of suffering and injustice has led Dawkins and many others to question the existence of a benevolent deity (i.e., theodicy).[6]

Dawkins applies the principle of Occam's Razor to God's existence, suggesting that more straightforward explanations of anything are generally better than more complex ones.[7] From this perspective, invoking the existence of a deity to explain the universe adds unnecessary complexity without providing satisfactory answers. Then there is the complex question that if God exists, then who made God?[8]

Dawkins also explored the cultural and psychological factors that contribute to religious belief, such as upbringing, socialization, and fear of death.[9] He argued that religious beliefs can be better understood as natural phenomena arising from human psychology and culture rather than divine revelation.[10]

Future of God—Biology

Regarding the future of faith in God, the field of biology does not have many scholars researching and writing on this topic. However, one did—Dawkins—so his writing tends to reflect the field. He found that God's existence is not something hard sciences can prove. Given that God cannot be proven using the scientific method, there can be no future of God.

---

6. Dawkins, *God Delusion*, 135.

7. Dawkins, *God Delusion*, 147–50.

8. Dawkins, *God Delusion*, 136.

9. Kardong also observed that religion helps people face death. Kardong, *Beyond God*, 17,

10. Dawkins, *God Delusion*, 208–21.

Evolution of God—Physics

PHYSICS IS THE STUDY of matter, energy, and force and how they operate in space and time. Basically, physics seeks to understand the basic laws and principles governing the universe. It is considered a hard science like biology. Some famous physicists include Albert Einstein, Stephen Hawking, Marie Curie, and Isaac Newton.

The relationship between physics and the concept of God has been debated by theologians, philosophers, and scientists for centuries. It involves both research into the nature of the universe and considerations about the existence of a divine being. According to Wright, "The coming of modern science has undermined the idea of gods and threatened the prospect of religion."[1]

Some theologians and philosophers perceive the big bang as evidence of a creation event orchestrated by a divine entity (a theory known as intelligent design). Some physicists believe that only a divine entity could set the fundamental constants and parameters in the universe to allow life to exist. One of these physicists is Peter Bussey, a professor of particle physics at the University of Glasgow. Bussey stated, "Our universe is in a very real sense 'fine-tuned' for our human existence. A substantial number of physical parameters . . . have values that are

---

1. Wright, *Evolution of God*, 67.

'right,' when there are very many more ways that their values could be 'wrong.' This certainly looks like purpose."[2]

However, others argue that scientific explanations suffice to describe the universe's origins. Dawkins countered the intelligent design argument with the *anthropic principle*. This principle states that if we are observing it, the universe evolved with the conditions necessary for intelligent life—or, the universe had to evolve in a way that led to our existence.[3] Simply, one could believe in either intelligent design or the anthropic principle.

A related idea is that the universe renews itself throughout time, starting with the big bang and collapsing back into a singularity (i.e., the "big crunch") only to initiate another big bang (reference figure 10). Eventually, one of the created universes would contain the correct parameters to create the universe that we exist in today. In such a scenario, God would have nothing to do with it, as this would be a natural aspect of the evolution of multiple universes. According to Monica Grady, professor of planetary and space science at the Open University,

> So how come all the physical laws and parameters in the universe happen to have the values that allowed stars, planets and ultimately life to develop? Some argue it's just a lucky coincidence. Others say we shouldn't be surprised to see biofriendly physical laws—they after all produced us, so what else would we see? Some theists, however, argue it points to the existence of a God creating favorable conditions. But God isn't a valid scientific explanation. The theory of the multiverse, instead, solves the mystery because it allows different universes to have different physical laws. So it's not surprising that we

---

2. Bussey, *Signposts to God*, 83.

3. Dawkins, *God Delusion*, 162–64. The anthropic principle comes in varying interpretations. These range from a simple description ("If we are here observing it, the universe evolved with the conditions necessary for the emergence of intelligent life") to something more radical ("The universe had to evolve in a way that led to our existence"). Sissa, "Designed for Life?"

should happen to see ourselves in one of the few universes that could support life.[4]

Bussey considered this scenario and rejected it, claiming, "Since there were no earlier times, an external cause for the universe is indicated, which we may choose to identify with a Creator."[5] However, science has not been able to determine what exactly existed before the very first big bang one way or the other—*as of now*. He acknowledged this, stating, "Claims that the cosmos is infinitely old are *at present* implausible."[6] So, it is equally reasonable to *not* choose to identify with a Creator.

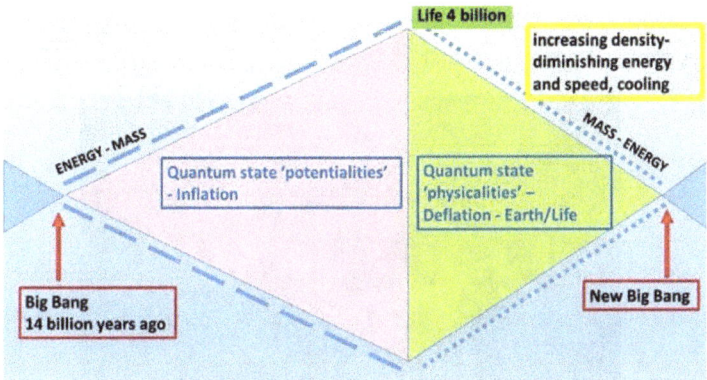

Figure 10: Schema of recurring big bang and life cycles[7]

Bussey also claims that because science cannot account for human consciousness, this is also evidence of the existence of God. He stated, "Physics cannot provide an account of human consciousness and hence human nature in its most central aspects."[8] However, this would seem plausible *if scientific progress ended today*.

4. Grady, "Laws of Physics."
5. Bussey, *Signposts to God*, 96.
6. Bussey, *Signposts to God*, 101; emphasis mine.
7. Reproduced by permission from Janecka, "Quantum State," 776, fig. 10.
8. Bussey, *Signposts to God*, 7.

The Future of God—Part 1

In contrast to Bussey, in a 2018 interview with Jamie Ducharme of *Time Magazine*, Stephen Hawking stated, "Before we understand science, it is natural to believe that God created the universe. But now science offers a more convincing explanation."[9] Hawking thought that all religions were based on faith and not on any factual evidence.

In his book *The Grand Design*, coauthored with Leonard Mlodinow, Hawking argued that the creation of the universe was a result of the laws of physics, not a divine creator. He wrote, "Because there is a law such as gravity, the universe can and will create itself from nothing. Spontaneous creation is the reason there is something rather than nothing, why the universe exists, why we exist."[10]

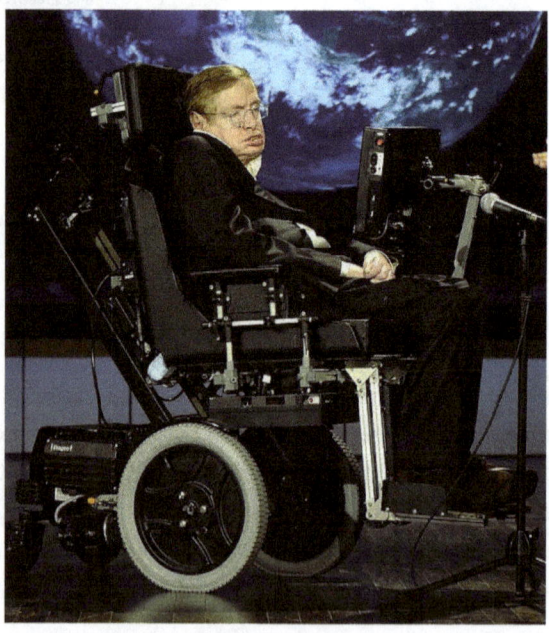

Figure 11: Stephen Hawking[11]

9. Ducharme, "Stephen Hawking."
10. Hawking and Mlodinow, *Grand Design*, 180.
11. Stephen Hawking photograph by NASA / Paul Alers, public domain, Wikimedia Commons.

Evolution of God—Physics

Regarding Bussey's belief that only God can explain how human beings have consciousness, Stephen Priest, a senior research fellow in philosophy at Oxford University, observed, "Interpretations of quantum physics presuppose the reality of consciousness. . . . Quantum reality depends on God's consciousness and the physical world depends on quantum reality. Therefore, the physical world depends on God's consciousness."[12] However, the relationship between quantum physics and consciousness remains controversial, and more research is needed to understand the connection between these two fields fully. Closely related to consciousness is the soul.

Souls and God

To begin, a soul is the immortal essence of a person. A person without a soul is considered dead.[13] The relationship, then, between souls and God is a central concept in many religious and philosophical traditions. In monotheistic religions, such as Christianity, Islam, and Judaism, the concept of the soul is often connected to the nature of God. In these religions, God is seen as the creator of all things, including human souls.[14] God endowed souls with qualities such as *consciousness*, morality, and free will. The relationship between souls and God is often depicted in terms of dependence, with souls ultimately accountable to God for their actions.[15]

In many religious traditions, the soul's destiny is closely linked to its relationship with God. Concepts of salvation,

12. Priest, "Quantum Physics," 1.

13. Wright stated, "Death is what happens when the soul departs a body for good." Wright, *Evolution of God*, 13. Unger was more succinct claiming, "Upon death, the body decomposes." Unger, *Religion of the Future*, 2.

14. "Then the LORD God formed a man from the dust of the ground and breathed into his nostrils the breath of life, and the man became a living being" (Gen 2:7).

15. "So then, each of us will give an account of ourselves to God" (Rom 14:12).

redemption, and spiritual liberation often revolve around the soul's journey toward union with God. For example, in Christianity, the doctrine of salvation through Jesus Christ emphasizes the reconciliation of souls with God through faith and redemption from sin.[16] Similarly, in Hinduism and Buddhism the goal of spiritual enlightenment involves transcending the cycle of birth, death, and rebirth (*samsara*) to achieve union with the divine or liberation (*moksha*).

Given the connection of souls to God, let's examine the viability of souls from a scientific perspective. To begin, Sean Carroll, a professor of philosophy at Johns Hopkins University, explained that in the quantum field theory, there is one field in the universe for each type of particle.[17] As such, if there was some life after death, then quantum tests would reveal such spirit or soul particles. They have not. This indicates that there is no way to allow the information in our brains (i.e., our souls) to persist after death. This means it is strictly a matter of faith whether or not souls exist.[18]

Turning to neuroscience, this is the only hard science field that directly researches souls. The development of fMRI techniques[19] has generated a boom in neuroscience research. Neuroscience continues to discover and account for the neural correlates of consciousness (NCC) within the brain.[20] Analogous to science diminishing the belief in God over time, the

---

16. "For God so loved the world that he gave his one and only Son, that whoever believes in him shall not perish but have eternal life" (John 3:16); "All this is from God, who reconciled us to himself through Christ and gave us the ministry of reconciliation: that God was reconciling the world to himself in Christ, not counting people's sins against them. And he has committed to us the message of reconciliation" (2 Cor 5:18–19).

17. Carroll, "Space Emerging."

18. Carroll, "Space Emerging."

19. Functional magnetic resonance imaging, or functional MRI (fMRI), measures brain activity by detecting changes associated with blood flow.

20. Neural correlates of consciousness refer to the specific neural activities that are associated with conscious experiences.

brain is replacing the soul as the prevailing explanation for the mind.[21]

Future of God—Physics

According to physics, the bottom line is that *when you die, you are dead*. Furthermore, there is no evidence of souls. As such, no souls are going to heaven to exist in the kingdom of God or to hell to mingle with the Devil. Wright concluded that many people today, particularly well-educated people, do not believe in an afterlife.[22] Hawking offered his perspective of an afterlife stating, "There is no heaven or afterlife. . . . That is a fairy story for people afraid of the dark."[23]

According to Grady, "Science requires proof, and religious belief requires faith. Scientists don't try to prove or disprove God's existence because they know there isn't an experiment that can ever detect God. And if you believe in God, it doesn't matter what scientists discover about the universe."[24]

Recap of Academic Perspectives

Up to this point, we briefly reviewed four primary academic fields (two soft sciences and two hard sciences)—theology, sociology, biology, and physics—to determine each one's general perspective on the future of God in Western societies. To begin, the bottom line regarding the future of God from the theological perspective is that God is becoming less and less essential to people's lives in modern societies. As the world modernizes, God is celebrated more culturally and historically, and less religiously.

21. Preston et al., "Neuroscience."
22. Wright, *Evolution of God*, 440.
23. Bowerman, "Heaven Is a Fairy Tale."
24. Grady, "If There Is a God."

The Future of God—Part 1

The trend in sociology supports growing secularism over religious persistence. Societies around the world are modernizing, which in turn has seen the downsizing of religion (e.g., the lowering attendance at church services) and of the belief in God. Also, the trend is towards a higher-educated population being more secular, which correlates to lower church participation and personal faith. Finally, the younger people are, the more likely they will not have the time or inclination to be religious. Conversely, older people today are more likely to remain religious to some degree due to religious persistence.

Regarding the future of faith in God, the field of biology cannot prove God's existence, which means there can be no future of God.

The bottom line in physics is that when you die, you are dead. Furthermore, souls cannot be proven to exist, so none are migrating to heaven, hell, or the kingdom of God. Finally, there is no future of God because God cannot be proven to exist.

Given the general conclusions of these academic fields, it seems that a revision of religion and faith in God is upon us. Armstrong concluded, "For 4,000 years religion has constantly adapted to meet the demands of the present, but in our own century, more and more people have found that it no longer works for them. Maybe God really is an idea of the past."[25] On the other hand, Durkheim observed that "religion obviously cannot play the same role in the future as it did in the past. However, religion seems destined to transform itself rather than disappear."[26] In fact, religious movements are born all the time. They compete with other faiths for followers to survive.[27]

---

25. Armstrong, *History of God*, 377.
26. Durkheim, *Elementary Forms*, 433.
27. Sumit, "Tomorrow's Gods."

PART 2

Future of God: It's Personal

FOR MANY DECADES NOW, perhaps even for centuries, humankind has increased its understanding of its surroundings (primarily through scientific discoveries) and correspondingly decreased its faith in God. As Shelby concluded, "The more we know and understand, the less necessary God becomes."[1] Smith also had a similar conclusion: "The more the universe seems comprehensible, the more religion seems pointless."[2] Armstrong observed, "People must outgrow God in their own good time."[3] According to a recent Pew Research study, over one-quarter of American adults now identify as religiously unaffiliated, compared to just 16 percent back in 2007. The unaffiliated (28 percent) now outnumber both Catholics (23 percent) and evangelical Protestants (24 percent).[4] The share of American adults who identify as religiously unaffiliated, known as "Nones," is now larger than any individual religious cohort.[5]

The millions of Nones are broken down into three main categories: agnostics (20 percent), atheists (17 percent), and

---

1. Shelby, *Evolution*, 212.
2. Smith, *Why Religion Matters*, 37.
3. Armstrong, *History of God*, 357.
4. Pew Research Center, "Religiously Unaffiliated."
5. DeRose, "Religious 'Nones.'"

The Future of God—Part 2

those who believe "nothing in particular" (63 percent).[6] Nones tend to be younger, Caucasian, and male.[7] Jason DeRose, the religion correspondent for National Public Radio News, reported in the *Washington Post*, "I think it's possible these people don't believe in anything [supernatural]. We just don't have the language [or religion] yet to describe what they do believe."[8]

However, it has been shown that believing in a higher power is healthier, at least mentally. The benefits outweigh the harm if one chooses to believe in God.[9] Finding solace in times of grief and loss is a human need. Religion and God have enabled the release of guilt by turning the grief over to a higher power.

There is no denying that religion taps into a psychological comfort zone.[10] Research shows that religious Americans (50 percent) are generally happier and less stressed than nonreligious Americans.[11] Shelby noted that as long as there is anxiety associated with our future, there is the potential for prayer and, therefore, belief in God.[12] One reason for this comfort with God is the fear of the unknown that is universal to human beings.[13] Another reason is that people need hope and comfort, and believing in God can provide that.[14]

Next, as we have witnessed with the fundamentalist movements in all three Abrahamic religions, many people are resistant to change. Limiting change is one of the primary

---

6. Pew Research Center, "Religiously Unaffiliated."

7. DeRose, "Religious 'Nones'"; My Air Force dog tag listed me as *None*—right below my blood type (I considered myself agnostic).

8. DeRose, "Religious 'Nones.'"

9. Shelby, *Evolution*, 40.

10. The supernatural is the only plausible source of things that humans desire. Shelby, *Evolution*, 45.

11. Shelby, *Evolution*, 49.

12. Shelby, *Evolution*, 191.

13. Shelby, *Evolution*, 51.

14. Shelby, *Evolution*, 45.

goals of religion.[15] So, as humankind evolves away from having faith and believing in God, it is clear that faith will probably never disappear, no matter how much science has discovered.[16] In 2022, a Pew poll found that almost half (45 percent) of the people surveyed affirmed that the United States should remain a "Christian Nation."[17]

Then, there is a political aspect to religious belief in that some political ideologies, primarily Communism, do not accept religion or the belief in God. As noted previously, Karl Marx (coauthor of the *Communist Manifesto*) considered religion to be the opiate of the masses to cope with their oppressed lives. In 1991, the Soviet Union, the original Communist country, dissolved into fifteen independent countries (none of which remained Communist). As such, many of the 290 million former Soviet citizens (mostly the younger ones) may have had no previous faith in a supernatural deity. Today, China is a communist country with over 1.4 billion citizens, many of whom also may have no faith in a supernatural deity. It would be fair to assume that some faithless people in the former Soviet Union and China would be amenable to believing in a deity (a total of over one and a half billion people combined).

Throughout history, religions have come and gone. When a religion dies, it tends to become a myth. New religions are often perceived as cults in the beginning, with most not surviving very long. The key to the survival of any new religion is an effective champion (such as the apostle Paul within Christianity) with a message that resonates with people (such as the belief that Jesus, as the Son of God, is the only way to get into heaven).[18]

---

15. Shelby, *Evolution*, 51.
16. Sumit, "Tomorrow's Gods."
17. *Washington Post*, "Nearly Half."
18. Sumit, "Tomorrow's Gods." Jesus declared, "I am the way and the truth and the life. No one comes to the Father except through me" (John 14:6). This verse emphasizes that belief in Jesus is the exclusive path to heaven.

The Future of God—Part 2

Finally, there is the impact of the Internet. Greg Cootsona, a professor of religious studies at California State University, Chico, reported that discussions on social media are largely hostile toward religious faith. Countless comments such as "the Internet will kill religion" and "Jesus will soon go the way of Zeus and Osiris" adversely affect the opinions of millions of Internet users regarding God and religion.[19]

New, Revised God

Armstrong concluded, "All our old conceptions of divinity had to die before theology could be reborn."[20] A new, revised religion is ripe to emerge at any time now. And, it should not require much faith as there is little appetite for it today, especially among the younger generations. Indeed, the fewer requirements a new religion has, the more likely it is to flourish in a modernizing world. As such, a new religion should be limited to *just one leap of faith*—the belief in a deity. However, the belief in an almighty deity that is all-knowing, ever-present, and all-powerful is, in fact, many leaps of faith. Therefore, as discussed earlier, this new, revised God would *not* be omnipotent, omniscient, and omnipresent. Indeed, the future of God could be a *personal* God tailored to each individual.

Having personal "Gods" also mitigates the suffering and evil issues addressed by theodicy. Mass evil events causing suffering could not be attributed to any personal God but more likely to scientific explanations.

Power of the Personal God

However, the definition of a deity implies powers that can affect a person. So, an individual's personal God could have

---

19. Cootsona, "Some Ways," 567.
20. Armstrong, *History of God*, 380.

some power to affect their life, but to what degree would be unknown. Furthermore, there is nothing a person can do to affect their personal God (i.e., more prayer or a sacrifice would not make the person's God more powerful). So, the one leap of faith is believing in a personal God with unknowable powers. Attributing any power to a personal God would be analogous to the Abrahamic religions' inherent sin or Hindu's postmortem karma (both concepts to be discussed shortly). It would inevitably lead to corruption and evil.

Reasons for Personal God

There are three main reasons for people to accept a personal God: joy, hope, and soulmate. Beginning with joy, having a personal God can enhance one's appreciation of nature, music, art, and buildings. This would be the divine feeling of awe that overwhelms a person when witnessing a religious icon, such as in the Sistine Chapel or Saint Paul's Cathedral, or when listening to an inspiring piece of music, such as Beethoven's *Ninth Symphony*. Such awe can cause people to change their core beliefs. Elliott Ihm (University of California, Santa Barbara) and Michiel van Elk (Leiden University) concluded in their 2020 research, "Experiences of awe may therefore play a prominent and perhaps fundamental role in religions."[21]

Next, if one has a personal god to pray to, this promotes hope, which is essential for mental health. As previously mentioned, praying has been determined to benefit a person's psychology.[22] Hope is essential for living life to the fullest. Redirecting one's efforts from the afterlife to the present should provide greater rewards and satisfaction.

Finally, having a soulmate aligns with human nature to be social. While everyone has different capacities for coping with isolation, having a personal God as a soulmate can help one

21. Ihm et al., "Awe," 146.
22. Shelby, *Evolution*, 45.

cope. Consider that solitary confinement for some prisoners is becoming illegal in many American states because it is considered cruel and unusual punishment.[23] The movie *Cast Away* was about a stranded mailman (played by actor Tom Hanks) on a deserted island who eventually humanizes a soccer ball, naming it "Wilson." With a personal God, this would not be necessary. Dawkins confirms this, writing that "we have a psychological need for God—imaginary friend, father, big brother, confessor, confidant—and the need has to be satisfied whether God really exists or not."[24]

Ramifications of One Leap of Faith

Just believing in a personal God means not believing in many religious tenets that have existed for millennia. There is no reason to believe in any afterlife, including heaven, hell, or the kingdom of God (as if God were a monarch). Atheists do not believe in any form of an afterlife. Instead, atheists believe that this life is the only one you get. Some atheists believe their death simply transforms their matter into energy or into something else. In any case, there may be some level of consciousness to this change. As a result, some atheists say that, upon death, they will become a part of the cosmic cycle through this transformation.[25]

Next, humankind's "inherent sin," the foundation of the Abrahamic religions, would not exist. Therefore, sin cannot be used as leverage to influence anything one does while alive. Analogous to this is that the reincarnation of souls also would

---

23. The Bureau of Justice Statistics announced in October 2015 that "in the United States penal system, upwards of 20 percent of state and federal prison inmates and 18 percent of local jail inmates are kept in solitary confinement at some point during their incarceration." Bureau of Justice Statistics, "Restrictive Housing."

24. Dawkins, *God Delusion*, 388.

25. American Atheists, "What Is Atheism?"; This transformation is similar to Buddhism.

not exist. Therefore, providing money, resources, and prayer to religious organizations would not affect anything for the provider after dying or for their ancestors who have already passed.

Additionally, karma would not apply to death. "One gets what one deserves" applies only while a person is alive. In other words, one's life is one's own responsibility. Nothing in life is predestined to happen (see "Open Theism"). That would be another leap of faith.

Historically, the leverage employed by organized religion using sin or karma to get people to do what they otherwise would not do is an important concept. To atone for one's inherent sins and those committed during one's lifetime, the Abrahamic religions ask for penance and prayer, often involving money. For example, during the Crusades, the pope granted crusading knights fighting on behalf of the church absolution of all sins (past, present, *and future*) and a guaranteed entrance into heaven.[26] (Many millions of innocent people were unnecessarily slaughtered during the Crusades.)

When a government aligns itself with a particular religion, its primary motivation is self-preservation—not the interests of its citizens.[27] Smith observed that "political leaders often use religion for their political ends."[28] A ruler also wants the legitimacy that the support of a popular religion provides.[29] Similarly, when a religion aligns with a state government, it is primarily for its own survival, which takes precedence over the survival of its followers.[30]

---

26. "Knights were especially attracted by what were effectively Get-Out-Of-Hell-Free cards allowing them to commit any sins throughout the rest of their lives without incurring liability in this or the next world." Medieval Warfare, "Crusades and Crusaders."

27. Shelby, *Evolution*, 22.

28. Smith, *Why Religion Matters*, 114.

29. A single powerful ruler requires a single powerful god to legitimize his rule. Sanderson, *Religious Evolution*, 195.

30. Shelby, *Evolution*, 211.

The Future of God—Part 2

When an organized religion teams up with a state government, the potential for evil arises. Kardong concluded that "both diplomacy and warfare are codified in and driven by religious practices."[31] We have seen this repeatedly throughout modern history, including the Christian Crusades, State Shinto in World War II, and Buddhist survivalist movements throughout Southeast Asia today. This marriage of politics and religion can result in political or military power abuse, including corruption. Unfortunately, Smith found that "there is no way to keep church and state separate."[32]

The best historical example of the corruption of money in the coordination of church and state involved the Knights Templar. This group had accumulated great wealth due to its security services and financial investments. In 1307, King Philip IV of France was in significant debt to the Knights. Instead of paying off the debt, he pressured Pope Clement V to arrest all of the Knights Templar. In 1312, the Catholic Church officially dissolved the Order of the Knights Templar and seized its assets. Dozens of knights, including their leader, Jacques de Molay, were subsequently tortured and burned at the stake for alleged heresy.[33]

Evolution of Faith in God

For thousands of years before Jesus Christ, historic societies believed in multiple gods (or divine entities), including the Greeks, Vikings, Romans, and American Indians. During the time of Christ, humankind's religious development eventually evolved into believing in only one almighty being, commonly referred to as "God/Yahweh/Allah." While most of the world's population today believes in just one god, multiple religions still believe in many "gods," such as Hinduism and Shinto. The

---

31. Kardong, *Beyond God*, 78.
32. Smith, *Why Religion Matters*, 121.
33. Masonic Vibe, "What Happened"; Kramer, "History of the Knights."

growth in the belief in one god corresponds with the diminishing belief in multiple gods.

Today, the religious evolution of the nature of God is occurring just as science is evolving. God may no longer be perceived as omnipotent, omnipresent, and all-knowing but rather as a personal confidant and supporter of the believer. According to Bellah, there is a deep human need to think of the universe and God as personal.[34] As noted earlier, Caputo declared that God is *within each person*.[35] This could be interpreted as each person having their own "God" for as long as they live. The evolution here is that when you die, you are dead, therefore your personal God would die with you. In summation, a person would still believe in one God; however, it would not be the same God for everyone. Rorty observed, "Religion is unobjectionable as long as long as it is privatized."[36] And, perhaps with personal gods, there would no longer be a need for churches.[37] Vattimo declared that the future of God and religion is the future of the church, and that the future of religion will depend on a position *beyond* atheism and theism.[38]

Accommodating a Personal God

Whitehead lectured about the three stages of humankind's relationship with God. It includes the transition from God the void, to God the enemy, to God the companion.[39] God the companion aligns with each person having a personal God. Furthering this line of thought, Wright observed, "Gods exist in people's heads."[40] A personal God is more like a sounding board or su-

---

34. Bellah, *Religion*, 104.
35. Caputo, *Folly of God*, 114.
36. Rorty and Vattimo, *Future of Religion*, 33.
37. Rorty and Vattimo, *Future of Religion*, 69.
38. Rorty and Vattimo, *Future of Religion*, 80.
39. Whitehead, *Religion in the Making*.
40. Wright, *Evolution of God*, 444.

pernatural best friend. (Remember, this human urge to believe in God is what sociologists refer to as *persistence*.)

It would also be the easiest religion to adopt as all world religions have tenets and rules one must believe in. The three Abrahamic religions have numerous policies and beliefs one should follow. For example, Kardong claimed that religious dietary laws are practiced enthusiastically because they give life purpose and focus.[41] However, these policies also represent religious burdens that can make living more challenging. Many of these policies were developed to protect the health and welfare of followers at that time. Today, we know a lot more than we did back then, so these policies are more customary and traditional than practical. Let's briefly review some of the customs and traditions of the Abrahamic religions that the faithful are asked to follow today.

Judaism Traditions

To begin, according to the Bible, a body is merely on loan by God and, therefore, must be kept virtuous and healthy. This is the reason why Jews are forbidden to mark their bodies with tattoos and multiple piercings. Leviticus 19:28 states explicitly, "Do not cut your bodies for the dead or put tattoo marks on yourselves." Ancient peoples of the Middle East demonstrated grief regarding the deities they worshiped by mutilating their bodies. Many would cut their skin to create a tattoo representing their deity, as well. Jews were forbidden from participating in these rituals as they represented pagan worship. The primary reason for this prohibition was likely the threat of infection and disease. Today, most Jews still hold that piercings and tattoos are prohibited.[42]

Judaism's most well-known restrictions have to do with food. *Kashrut* is a Jewish law that deals with what foods can and

---

41. Kardong, *Beyond God*, 243.
42. Jewish Virtual Library, "Issues in Jewish Ethics."

cannot be eaten and how those foods must be prepared. The word *kosher* describes food that meets the standards of *kashrut*. Examples of *kashrut* include the following:

- Only approved animals may be eaten. Then, those that can be eaten must be killed according to Jewish tradition.
- Only certain animal parts may be eaten.
- Meat cannot be eaten with dairy. Fish, eggs, fruits, vegetables, and grains can be eaten with either meat or dairy.
- Utensils used with meat may not be used with dairy, and vice versa.
- Utensils used with non-kosher food may not be used with kosher food.[43]

Regarding the Jewish tradition of treating illnesses, Jewish scholars debate the form of treatment because, according to the Bible, illness is considered a form of divine punishment. If doctors treat and cure the Jewish patient, then they may be contravening the will and plans of God.[44]

In biblical times, shaving one's face was considered a pagan practice. So, for Jewish men, shaving was prohibited (hence why most devout male Jews had full beards). Deuteronomy 22:5 states, "A woman must not wear men's clothing, nor a man wear women's clothing, for the LORD your God detests anyone who does this." This implies the Lord does not favor the sharing of gender customs. Rabbinic scholars determined that this included a man shaving his face (as women cannot grow beards).[45]

Circumcision is a procedure that removes the foreskin from a baby boy's penis. It is one of the most ancient practices of Judaism. The Torah requires the circumcision of male babies.[46]

---

43. Jewish Virtual Library, "Jewish Dietary Laws."
44. Jewish Virtual Library, "Healthy Body and Soul."
45. Jewish Virtual Library, "Beards."
46. Gen 17:7–14 and repeated in Lev 12:3.

The reason for this was to satisfy a covenant with God. However, it also was an effective way to prevent the transmission of diseases during intercourse.[47] Kardong offers his bottom line on Judaism's restrictions stating, "Today no practical reasons remain to observe taboos at all."[48]

Christian Traditions

The Bible expressly forbids many things that serve as a basis for Christian traditions. To begin, according to Deut 18:10–11, "Let no one be found among you who sacrifices their son or daughter in the fire, who practices divination or sorcery, interprets omens, engages in witchcraft, or casts spells, or who is a medium or spiritist or who consults the dead." Some of these practices involve the invocation of supernatural powers other than God, which goes against Christian beliefs.

Exodus 20:14 states, "You shall not commit adultery." Adultery refers to having sexual relations outside of marriage, which Christianity has always condemned. Premarital sex is also considered sinful, as the Bible instructs followers to refrain from sexual immorality and honor marriage.[49] Engaging in casual sex before or outside marriage is seen as cheapening the divine gift of physical intimacy.

Gambling, though popular as a form of entertainment, is morally questionable according to most Christian authorities. The Bible cautions against it in several places because it can promote greed and enable addictive tendencies.[50] These are but a few examples of restrictions levied upon followers of Christianity.

---

47. Jewish Virtual Library, "Circumcision."
48. Kardong, *Beyond God*, 243.
49. Heb 13:4.
50. "For the love of money is a root of all kinds of evil. Some people, eager for money, have wandered from the faith and pierced themselves with many griefs" (1 Tim 6:10).

Islam Traditions

In Islam, one of the most well-known restrictions is food consumption. Muslim dietary law breaks down food and drink into two groups: permissible (*halal*) and not permissible (*haram*). Forbidden substances include pork, animals not slaughtered following Islamic guidelines, drugs, alcohol, animals without external ears, and the presence of blood in any product. At that time, pigs were perceived as carriers of diseases.[51]

Besides food, restrictions in Islam come from Sharia. Sharia is divine guidance whereas Islamic law represents the interpretation and application of Sharia. Sharia law is the most intrusive and restrictive in the world. It focuses on family matters, such as marriage, divorce, and inheritance.[52]

As modern society veers away from established religions and the historical "baggage" associated with them, a religion that features just one leap of faith and no baggage should appear appealing.

---

51. Dur-e-Sabih, "Muslim Dietary Restrictions."
52. Al-Yousef, "What Is Sharia Law?"

Conclusion

IF ANY RELIGION IN world history were perfect, we would not witness the denominational branching or sects continually being created.[1] In other words, no single religion has satisfied nor will satisfy everyone.[2] New denominational branches are motivated by many factors, including greed (specifically money) and political power (specifically corruption). An early example of a new denominational branch was the Cathars (now extinct), a branch of Christianity that rejected the idea of confession, baptism, and the Holy Eucharist.[3]

Another key reason for a new denominational branch is a new interpretation that appeals to people more than the current set of beliefs. Stark noted, "There must be something novel about the new religion in order to justify change," and that "people embraced a new faith because they find its teachings appealing."[4] The best example of this is the separation of Christianity from Judaism.

Change could evolve *from within* a religion such as Catholicism. As previously discussed, the pope could use several mechanisms to direct a change in religious doctrine or policy. However, getting Catholicism to move from one all-powerful

---

1. Shelby, *Evolution*, 52.
2. Shelby, *Evolution*, 65.
3. Stark, *Discovering God*, 56–57. The Inquisitions were initially established as a means to discourage Catharism.
4. Stark, *Discovering God*, 51, 199.

and all-knowing God to just one personal God for each follower would take the longest time of any of the evolution possibilities—though it is possible.

The next possibility is for change to evolve from an established religion such as Protestantism. Because Protestants do not have one overarching leader like the Catholics do (i.e., the pope), branches can and have occurred emphasizing different beliefs and interpretations. Shelby observed, "The division of the Christian faith involved several political issues primarily as a result of inherent vagueness and ambiguous translations from the original Hebrew into Greek and Latin."[5] Major Protestant branches include evangelicals, Southern Baptists, Lutherans, Presbyterians, and Methodists.

Finally, a new religion could evolve from an original source, such as the ancient faiths. Stark observed that "all successful new religions are founded by gifted individuals."[6] With the continued loss of faith around the world, one day it may be possible that the only faith remaining is just the belief in one personal deity.

For thousands of years, humankind believed in multiple gods or almighty deities. Eventually, the belief in one almighty deity took hold in the Middle East. Judaism solidified this belief, which subsequently transferred to Christianity and then again to Islam. Today, the majority of the earth's population believes in one God. It appears that humankind is on the verge of further religious evolution—the belief in just one life and one personal God. This evolution accommodates the continued scientific advancements characteristic of modern societies.

---

5. Shelby, *Evolution*, 56.
6. Stark, *Discovering God*, 156. See appendix on Monysm.

Appendix

Monysm

I WOULD LIKE TO propose a new religion for Nones, former Communists, highly-educated people, and modernists to consider. *Monysm* would be the name of the proposed religion. This new religion would be founded on the tenet "One leap of faith"—that of a personal God. As such, it makes sense to call it "Monism." However, that word already has a meaning: "The metaphysical and theological view that all is one, that there are no fundamental divisions, and that a unified set of laws underlie all of nature."[1] This is the reason the proposed minimalist religion could be "Monysm," for which there is no other word meaning. As such, followers of Monysm could be referred to as Monysts. And, the study of Monysm could be called Monysticism.

God is capitalized because each person's personal God has unknowable power that can affect the Monyst or anyone or anything else, as prayed for by the Monyst.

Monysm would be founded upon the philosophical belief that sentient beings live and exist only once. This accommodates the physics determination that when you die, you are dead.

---

1. Basics of Philosophy, "Monism."

The Future of God

Monysm should not be an organized religion or institution; it should primarily be a shared belief. As such, Monysts may want to pray together and share spiritual experiences with one another. This socializing can be done by congregating in public areas such as libraries or parks. (This prevents having to rent space, which would necessitate the management of money.)

Tenets of Monysm

Monysts are encouraged to pray to their personal God whenever and wherever they choose.

Monyst leaders are volunteers and should receive no financial contributions—much like monks or Imams.

There should only be as much organization as needed to facilitate social gatherings of Monysts.

Monysm does not require rituals, customs, or sacrifices of any kind.

While Monysm can be proselytized around the world, it should not be done violently. It does not condone violence of any kind at any time for any reason.

Monysm should never be officially affiliated with politics or government.

There is no correlation between how powerful personal Gods are and how many prayers are made to them. (How powerful a personal God is cannot be known.)

One's consciousness is internal (to oneself) while a personal God is external.

All Monysts have equal standing.

It is a leap of faith to believe a Monyst's personal God can communicate with anyone other than the Monyst. One's personal God can only hear the believer.

It is a leap of faith to believe one's personal God can communicate with other personal Gods. Personal Gods do not communicate or work together.

Bibliography

Ackroyd, P. R., and C. F. Evans, eds. *From the Beginnings to Jerome*. Vol. 1 of *The Cambridge History of the Bible*. Cambridge: Cambridge University Press, 1970.

Ahmed, Nazeer. "Ghazan the Great." History of Islam. https://historyofislam.com/ghazan-the-great/.

Alim. "The Kharijite Plot." https://www.alim.org/history/khalifa-ali/martyrdom-of-ali-661-c-e-/#section1.

Al-Yousef, Hassan. "What Is Sharia Law?" Islam Laws, Mar. 5, 2025. https://islam-laws.com/what-is-sharia-law/.

American Atheists. "What Is Atheism?" https://www.atheists.org/activism/resources/about-atheism/.

American Sociological Association. "What Is Sociology?" https://www.asanet.org/about/what-is-sociology/.

Andrews, Mikkel. "How Old Was Mary When She Had Jesus?" Bible Scripture, Nov. 21, 2024. https://biblescripture.net/how-old-was-mary-when-she-had-jesus-historical-biblical-insights/.

Armstrong, Karen. *A History of God*. New York: Ballantine, 1993.

———. *The Role of Religion in Today's Conflict*. New York: UN Alliance of Civilizations, 2006. https://www.unaoc.org/repository/Armstrong_Religion_Conflict.pdf.

Aslan, Reza. *God: A Human History*. New York: Random House, 2017.

Banerjee, Neela. "Poll Finds a Fluid Religious Life in U.S." *New York Times*, Feb. 26, 2008. https://www.nytimes.com/2008/02/26/us/26religion.html.

Basics of Philosophy. "Monism." https://www.philosophybasics.com/branch_monism.html.

BBC News. "Israel Country Profile." Last modified Oct. 13, 2023. https://www.bbc.com/news/world-middle-east-14628835.

Bellah, Robert. *Religion in Human Evolution: From the Paleolithic to the Axial Age*. Cambridge: Harvard University Press, 2011.

Berlin, Adele. *Poetics and Interpretation of Biblical Narrative*. University Park, PA: Eisenbrauns, 1994.

Bibliography

Bhadauria, Devanshu. "Max Weber: Theory of Religion." *Research Journal of Humanities and Social Sciences* 3 (2012) 17–22. https://rjhssonline.com/HTMLPaper.aspx?Journal=Research%20Journal%20of%20Humanities%20and%20Social%20Sciences;PID=2012-3-1-5.

Blankinship, Khalid Yahya. *The End of the Jihad State: The Reign of Hisham Ibn 'Abd-al Malik and the Collapse of the Umayyads*. New York: State University of New York Press, 1994.

Bowerman, Mary. "Heaven Is a Fairy Tale." *USA Today*, Mar. 14, 2018. https://www.usatoday.com/story/tech/nation-now/2018/03/14/heaven-fairy-story-what-stephen-hawking-says-happens-when-people-die/423344002/.

Brinkmann, Tobias. "Jewish Migration." EGO, Dec. 3, 2010. https://ieg-ego.eu/en/threads/europe-on-the-road/jewish-migration.

Brown, Candy Gunther, and Mark Silk, eds. *The Future of Evangelicalism in America*. New York: Columbia University Press, 2016.

Bureau of Justice Statistics. "Use of Restrictive Housing in U.S. Prisons and Jails, 2011–12." Oct. 23, 2015. https://bjs.ojp.gov/press-release/use-restrictive-housing-us-prisons-and-jails-2011-12.

Bussey, Peter. *Signposts to God: How Modern Physics and Astronomy Point the Way to Belief*. Lisle, IL: IVP Academic, 2016.

Butler, Alfred J. *The Arab Conquest of Egypt and the Last Thirty Years of the Roman Dominion*. Oxford: Oxford University Press, 1978.

Camilleri, Adrian. "Aquinas: Theodicy and Free Will." PhilosophyMT, Sept. 2, 2023. https://philosophymt.com/aquinas-theodicy-and-free-will/.

Campbell, Douglas A. "The Future of New Testament Theology, or, What Should Devout Modern Bible Scholarship Look Like?" *Religions* 12 (2021) 1072. https://doi.org/10.3390/rel12121072.

Caputo, John D. *The Folly of God: A Theology of the Unconditional*. Salem, OR: Polebridge, 2016.

Carroll College. "Vatican II." https://www.carroll.edu/about/history/catholic-history-heritage/vatican-ii.

Carroll, Sean. "Space Emerging from Quantum Mechanics." In Truth Only Atoms and the Void (blog), July 18, 2016. https://www.preposterousuniverse.com/blog/2016/07/18/space-emerging-from-quantum-mechanics/.

Cartwright, Mark. "Black Death." World History Encyclopedia, Apr. 5, 2023. https://www.worldhistory.org/Black_Death/.

Catholic Arena. "10 Papal Encyclicals That Every Catholic Should Read." Nov. 15, 2020. https://www.catholicarena.com/latest/papalencyclicals.

Catholic Bridge. "The 21 Ecumenical Councils of the Catholic Church." https://www.catholicbridge.com/catholic/21-catholic-councils.php.

Cavendish, Richard. "The Mongols." *History Today* 58.2 (2008). https://www.historytoday.com/archive/months-past/baghdad-sacked-mongols.

Chakra, Hayden. "The Rise and Fall of the Abbasid Dynasty." About History, Apr. 26, 2023. https://about-history.com/the-rise-and-fall-of-the-abbasid-dynasty/.

Bibliography

Chopra, Deepak. *The Future of God*. New York: Harmony, 2014.

ChurchTrac. "The State of Church Attendance: Trends and Statistics (2025)." https://www.churchtrac.com/articles/the-state-of-church-attendance-trends-and-statistics-2023.

Conway, Daniel. "Exemplarity and Its Discontents: On the Hegelian Futures of Religion." *Owl of Minerva* 52 (2021) 137–57. https://doi.org/10.5840/owl20216238.

Coogan, Michael. *The Old Testament: A Very Short Introduction*. Oxford: Oxford University Press, 2008.

Cootsona, Greg. "Some Ways Emerging Adults Are Shaping the Future of Religion and Science." *Zygon* 51 (2016) 557–72. https://doi.org/10.1111/zygo.12270.

Corcuera, Bob. "The Abbasid Revolution." Exploring History, Jan. 31, 2018. https://exploringhist.blogspot.com/2018/01/the-abbasid-revolution.html.

Crossman, Ashley. "Sociology of Religion." ThoughtCo, July 3, 2019. https://www.thoughtco.com/sociology-of-religion-3026286.

Dawkins, Richard. *The God Delusion*. Boston: Mariner, 2008.

———. "When Religion Steps on Science's Turf." *Free Inquiry* 18.2 (1998) 18–19. https://cdn.centerforinquiry.org/wp-content/uploads/sites/26/1998/04/22155918/p18.pdf.

DeRose, Jason. "Religious 'Nones' Are Now the Largest Single Group in the U.S." NPR, Jan. 24, 2024. https://www.npr.org/2024/01/24/1226371734/religious-nones-are-now-the-largest-single-group-in-the-u-s.

Ducharme, Jamie. "Stephen Hawking Was an Atheist: Here's What He Said About God, Heaven and His Own Death." *Time*, Mar. 14, 2018. https://time.com/5199149/stephen-hawking-death-god-atheist/.

Dur-e-Sabih. "Muslim Dietary Restrictions: Everything You Need to Know." Muslim Dietician, Jan. 24, 2023. https://amuslimdietitian.com/muslim-dietary-restrictions-everything-you-need-to-know-guest/.

Durkheim, Émile. *The Elementary Forms of Religious Life*. New York: Free Press, 1912.

Easy Sociology. "Islamic Fundamentalism: An Introduction." Oct. 25, 2024. https://easysociology.com/sociology-of-religion/islamic-fundamentalism-an-introduction/.

Encyclopedia Britannica. "Hasan." Last modified Mar. 20, 2025. https://www.britannica.com/biography/Hasan.

Evangelical Lutheran Church in America. *Constitution, Bylaws, and Continuing Resolutions of the Metropolitan Chicago Synod of the Evangelical Lutheran Church in America*. Presented and approved at the 2022 Synod Assembly of the Metropolitan Chicago Synod, Nov. 2022. https://mcselca.org/wp-content/uploads/Current-MCS-Constitution-June-2023-FINAL-updated30.pdf.

Evely, Bob. *At the End of Ages: The Abolition of Hell*. Self-published, 1stBooks Library, 2003.

Evers, Dirk, et al., eds. *Is Religion Natural?* Edinburgh: T & T Clark, 2012.

Bibliography

A Faithful Version. "The Canonization of the Old Testament." https://afaithfulversion.org/commentary-canonization/.

Farhan, Roshan. "Evolving Beliefs: The Impact of Secularization on Modern Religious Practice and Identity." *Sociology and Criminology* 12 (2024) 319. https://www.longdom.org/open-access-pdfs/evolving-beliefs-the-impact-of-secularization-on-modern-religious-practice-and-identity.pdf.

FECYT Spanish Foundation for Science and Technology. "Religious Beliefs Seen as Basis of Origins of Paleolithic Art." ScienceDaily, Apr. 19, 2010. https://www.sciencedaily.com/releases/2010/03/100326101115.htm.

Flem-Ath, Rand. "Moses: Myth, Fiction or History?" Ancient Origins, last modified Dec. 31, 2023. https://www.ancient-origins.net/history-famous-people/moses-myth-or-history-002246.

4 Marks of the Church. "Early Church Councils." 2020. https://4marksofthechurch.com/church-history-list-of-early-councils/.

Fradd, Matt. "4 Times Mormonism Changed Its Doctrine." *Pints with Aquinas*. https://pintswithaquinas.com/4-times-mormonism-changed-its-doctrine/.

Francis. *Fiducia Supplicans: On the Pastoral Meaning of Blessings*. Vatican, Dec. 18, 2023. https://www.vatican.va/roman_curia/congregations/cfaith/documents/rc_ddf_doc_20231218_fiducia-supplicans_en.html.

Galan, S. "Number of Pupils in Primary Education Worldwide from 2000 to 2023." Statista, Mar. 8, 2025. https://www.statista.com/statistics/1227106/number-of-pupils-in-primary-education-worldwide/.

Galbraith, Deane. "When Jesus Was Alive, Resurrections Were Commonplace." *Otago Daily Times*, Apr. 14, 2022. https://www.odt.co.nz/opinion/when-jesus-was-alive-resurrections-were-commonplace.

Gallup. "How Many Americans Believe in God?" Last modified June 24, 2022. https://news.gallup.com/poll/268205/americans-believe-god.aspx.

———. "Religion." https://news.gallup.com/poll/1690/Religion.aspx.

Giuliano, Paola, and Nathan Nunn. "Understanding Cultural Persistence and Change." Cambridge, MA: National Bureau of Economic Research, 2017. https://scholar.harvard.edu/files/nunn/files/tradition_paper_v8.pdf.

Gobry, Pascal-Emmanuel. "Why Religion Will Dominate the 21st Century." *Week*, Feb. 10, 2016. https://theweek.com/articles/555371/why-religion-dominate-21st-century.

Goodfriend, Elaine. "Why Is the Torah Divided into Five Books?" Torah. https://www.thetorah.com/article/why-is-the-torah-divided-into-five-books.

Gould, Stephen Jay. *Rocks of Ages: Science and Religion in the Fullness of Life*. New York: Ballantine, 1999.

Grady, Monica. "Can the Laws of Physics Disprove God?" The Conversation, Feb. 22, 2021. https://theconversation.com/can-the-laws-of-physics-disprove-god-146638.

———. "If There Is a God, Would They Be Bound by the Laws of Physics?" BBC, Mar. 1, 2021. https://www.stage.bbc.co.uk/future/article/20210301-how-physics-could-prove-god-exists.

Bibliography

Grammich, Clifford A. "Catholics in the U.S." US Religious Census, Nov. 2022. https://www.usreligioncensus.org/sites/default/files/2023-05/RRA%20Catholic%20presentation.pdf.

Greeley, Andrew. *The Persistence of Religion*. London: SCM, 1973. https://www-cambridge-org.proxy.ccis.edu/core/journals/new-blackfriars/article/persistence-of-religion-by-andrew-greeley-scm-press-london-1973-280-pp-280/EEDA20665DA41845F4D331338761DA9C.

Grimshaw, Mike. "Radical Theologies." *Palgrave Communications* 1 (2015). https://www.nature.com/articles/palcomms201532.

Hameed, Salman. "Dennett and Problems with Gould's NOMA." Irtiqa, Aug. 20, 2008. https://www.irtiqa-blog.com/2008/08/dennett-and-problems-with-goulds-noma.html.

Harden, John A. "The Concept of Miracle from St. Augustine to Modern Apologetics." *Theological Studies* 15 (1954) 229–57. https://theologicalstudies.net/wp-content/uploads/2022/11/Hardon-Concept-of-Miracle-Augustine-to-Modern.pdf.

Haught, John F. *What Is Religion? An Introduction*. Mahwah, NJ: Paulist, 1990.

Hawking, Stephen, and Leonard Mlodinow. *The Grand Design*. New York: Bantam, 2010.

Hemmings, Jay. "When the Egyptian Mamluks Crushed the Formerly Unstoppable Mongol Army." War History Online, Feb. 28, 2019. https://www.warhistoryonline.com/instant-articles/the-battle-of-ayn-jalut.html.

History Guild. "The Umayyad and Abbasid Empire." https://historyguild.org/the-umayyad-and-abbasid-empire/.

History Lists. "List of 9 Crusades to the Holy Land." https://historylists.org/events/9-crusades-into-the-holy-land.html.

History of Christian Theology. "Christianity in the First and Second Century: Growth, Persecution and Transformation." https://historyofchristiantheology.com/commentary/period-i-early-and-medieval-church/christianity-in-the-first-and-second-century/.

Hornborg, Alf. "Animism, Fetishism, and Objectivism as Strategies for Knowing (or Not Knowing) the World." *Ethnos* 71 (2006) 21–32. https://doi.org/10.1080/00141840600603129.

Hurst, Gordon. "The Abbasid Caliphate." Hurst History. https://www.hursthistory.org/uploads/1/0/7/0/107013873/abbasid_caliphate.pdf.

Ihm, Elliott, et al. "Awe as a Meaning-Making Emotion." In *The Evolution of Religion, Religiosity and Theology*, edited by Jay Feierman and Lluis Oviedo, 134–50. New York: Routledge, 2019.

Iraqi Dinar US Rates News. "The Iran-Iraq War: Reason and Timeline of the Conflict." Jan. 19, 2024. https://www.iraqidinarusd.com/2024/01/the-iran-iraq-war-reason-and-timeline.html.

Islamic Finder. "Short Biography of Ali Ibn Talib (R.A.)." https://www.islamicfinder.org/knowledge/biography/story-of-ali-ibn-talib-ra/.

Bibliography

Janecka, Ivo P. "From a Quantum State to a Quantum State. *Life as a Temporary Emergence of a Differentiated Physicality*." *American Journal of Educational Research* 7 (2019) 764–79.

Jerusalem Post Staff. "72% of Israelis Say Country Failed to Learn Lessons of Oct. 7, Tensions Between Jews and Arabs." *Jerusalem Post*, Jan. 30, 2025. https://www.jpost.com/israel-news/article-840006.

Jesus Everyday. "What Is 'Ecumenical Council' in the Catholic Church?" https://www.jesus-everyday.com/what-is-ecumenical-council-in-the-catholic-church/.

Jewish History. "The Men of the Great Assembly." https://www.jewishhistory.org/the-men-of-the-great-assembly/.

Jewish Virtual Library. "Ancient Jewish History: The Bar-Kokhba Revolt." https://www.jewishvirtuallibrary.org/the-bar-kokhba-revolt-132–135-ce.

———. "Ancient Jewish History: The Great Revolt." https://www.jewishvirtuallibrary.org/the-great-revolt-66–70-ce.

———. "Issues in Jewish Ethics: Tattoos." https://www.jewishvirtuallibrary.org/tattoos-in-judaism.

———. "Jewish Dietary Laws (Kashrut): Overview of Laws and Regulations." https://www.jewishvirtuallibrary.org/overview-of-jewish-dietary-laws-and-regulations.

———. "Jewish Practices and Rituals: A Healthy Body and Soul." https://www.jewishvirtuallibrary.org/a-healthy-body-and-soul.

———. "Jewish Practices and Rituals: Beards." https://www.jewishvirtuallibrary.org/beards.

———. "Jewish Practices and Rituals: Circumcision—Brit Milah." https://www.jewishvirtuallibrary.org/circumcision-brit-milah.

Kardong, Kenneth. *Beyond God: Evolution and the Future of Religion*. Amherst, NY: Humanity, 2010.

Khalaji, Mehdi. "Iran's Anti-Western 'Blueprint' for the Next Fifty Years." Washington Institute, Oct. 24, 2018. https://www.washingtoninstitute.org/policy-analysis/irans-anti-western-blueprint-next-fifty-years.

Khan, Syed. "Abbasid Dynasty." World History Encyclopedia, Jan. 28, 2020. https://www.worldhistory.org/Abbasid_Dynasty/.

———. "Umar." World History Encyclopedia, Jan. 23, 2020. https://www.worldhistory.org/Umar/.

———. "Umayyad Dynasty." World History Encyclopedia, Jan. 28, 2020. https://www.worldhistory.org/Umayyad_Dynasty/.

Khosa, Aasha. "Ijtihad Makes Muslim Societies Adapt to the Changing Times." Awaz The Voice, June 6, 2023. https://www.awazthevoice.in/society-news/ijtihad-makes-muslim-societies-adapt-to-the-changing-times-22110.html.

Killen, Patricia, and Mark Silk, eds. *The Future of Catholicism in America*. Columbia: Columbia University Press, 2019.

Bibliography

Kirch, Joseph. "Vatican Council: The Question of Papal Infallibility." *The Catholic Encyclopedia.* Vol. 15. New York: Robert Appleton, 1912. http://www.newadvent.org/cathen/15303a.htm.

Knight, Christopher C. "The Evolution of Religiosity: A Theologian's View." In *The Evolution of Religion, Religiosity and Theology,* edited by Jay Feierman and Lluis Oviedo, 190-204. New York: Routledge, 2019.

Kohler, Pam. "Israel: What Does the Future Hold?" Salvation and Survival, Mar. 18, 2015. https://www.salvationandsurvival.com/2015/03/israel.html?m=0.

Kokkinidis, Tasos. "The Ancient Greek Jesus Christ, Apollonius of Tyana." Greek Reporter, Apr. 18, 2025. https://greekreporter.com/2025/04/18/greek-jesus-christ-apollonius-tyana/.

Kramer, Gabrielle. "The History of the Knights Templar: From Inception to Downfall." History Hit, June 27, 2018. https://www.historyhit.com/who-were-the-knights-templar/.

Kristof, Nicholas. "America Is Losing Religious Faith." *New York Times,* Aug. 24, 2023. https://www.nytimes.com/2023/08/23/opinion/christianity-america-religion-secular.html.

Lapidus, Ira M. *A History of Islamic Societies.* Cambridge: Cambridge University Press, 2002.

Lataster, Raphael. "Did Historical Jesus Really Exist? The Evidence Just Doesn't Add Up." Church and State, Dec. 15, 2015. https://churchandstate.org.uk/2015/12/did-historical-jesus-really-exist-the-evidence-just-doesnt-add-up/.

Latham, Andrew. "The Crusades: A Very Brief History, 1095-1500." Medievalists. https://www.medievalists.net/2025/03/crusades-history-1095-1500/.

Lemonick, Michael D. "Are the Bible's Stories True? Archaeology's Evidence." *Time,* Dec. 18, 1995. https://time.com/archive/6728313/are-the-bibles-stories-true-archaeologys-evidence/.

Library of Congress. "From Haven to Home: 350 Years of Jewish Life in America." https://www.loc.gov/exhibits/haventohome/haven-century.html.

Lloyd-Moffet, Stephen. "The Future of Religion." Presentation to the Unitarian Universalist Community of Cambria in 2019. Posted Apr. 19, 2019. Video, 35:57. https://www.youtube.com/watch?v=hYKBFUHpMgQ.

Mamun, Mohammad. "Hazrat Uthman Ibn Affan (RA)." Islamic Info Center, Oct. 26, 2024. https://islamicinfocenter.com/hazrat-uthman-ibn-affan/.

Mark, Joshua. "Canaan." World History Encyclopedia, Oct. 23, 2018. https://www.worldhistory.org/canaan/.

Masonic Vibe. "What Happened to the Knights Templar on Friday the 13th." Mar. 30, 2023. https://masonicvibe.com/the-knights-templar-on-friday-the-13th/.

Bibliography

Matsuura, Koïchiro. "Ending Poverty Through Education: The Challenge of Education for All." *UN Chronicle* 44.4 (2007). https://www.un.org/en/chronicle/article/ending-poverty-through-education-challenge-education-all.

McMahon, Robert, ed. "The Sunni-Shia Divide." Council of Foreign Affairs, Apr. 27, 2023. https://www.cfr.org/article/sunni-shia-divide.

Mead, George Herbert. *Mind, Self, and Society from the Standpoint of a Social Behaviorist*. Chicago: University of Chicago Press, 1934. https://ia903102.us.archive.org/18/items/MEADGeorgeSelfMindAndSociety/MEAD%2C%20George-%20Self%2C%20Mind%20and%20Society.pdf.

Meador, Jake. "The Misunderstood Reason Millions of Americans Stopped Going to Church." *Atlantic*, July 29, 2023. https://www.theatlantic.com/ideas/archive/2023/07/christian-church-communitiy-participation-drop/674843/.

Medieval Warfare. "Crusades and Crusaders." https://www.medievalwarfare.info/crusades.htm.

Mello-Klein, Cody. "Science and Religion Can Get Along, Says Former Director of the National Institutes of Health." Northeastern Global News, Apr. 13, 2024. https://news.northeastern.edu/2024/04/09/science-religion-francis-collins/.

Messier, Kathleen. "Hear Ye, One and All: The Papal Bull." *Vermont Catholic*, June 30, 2023. https://www.vermontcatholic.org/vermont/hear-ye-one-and-all-the-papal-bull/.

Miller, George. "The Cognitive Revolution: A Historical Perspective." *Trends in Cognitive Sciences* 7.3 (2003) 141–44. https://www.cs.princeton.edu/~rit/geo/Miller.pdf.

Mostert, Christiaan. *God and the Future*. London: T & T Clark, 2002.

Mozumder, Mohammad. "Interrogating Post-Secularism: Jürgen Habermas, Charles Taylor, and Talal Asad." Master's thesis, University of Pittsburg, 2011. https://d-scholarship.pitt.edu/6878/1/MohammadMozumder2011MAThesis.pdf.

Nasr, Seyyed Hossein. *Islam: Religion, History and Civilization*. New York: HarperCollins, 2003.

Nelson-Goedert, Nicholaus. "The Power of Socialization: How It Shapes Our Lives." Sociology Inc, May 25, 2023. https://sociologyinc.com/the-power-of-socialization-how-it-shapes-our-lives/.

Nelson-Pallmeyer, Jack. *Is Religion Killing Us?* New York: Continuum International, 2003.

NeuronUp. "Cognitive Abilities: What They Are, Types, Functioning and Stimulation." July 27, 2021. https://neuronup.us/cognitive-stimulation-news/cognitive-abilities-what-they-are-types-functioning-and-stimulation/.

Bibliography

New World Encyclopedia. "European Colonization of the Americas." https://www.newworldencyclopedia.org/entry/European_Colonization_of_the_Americas.

———. "Great Schism." https://www.newworldencyclopedia.org/entry/Great_Schism.

———. "Talmud." https://www.newworldencyclopedia.org/entry/Talmud.

Norelius, Per-Johan. "The Origins of Soul-Beliefs: A Survey of Theories from the 19th Century to the Present." In *Examining the Concept of the Soul*, edited by Leah Hawkins and Brent Bowers, 1–56. New York: Nova Science, 2018.

Norton, Nicole. "Where Is Christianity Currently Growing the Most?" NCESC, last modified June 21, 2024. https://www.ncesc.com/geographic-faq/where-is-christianity-currently-growing-the-most/.

NSCC. "The Hebrews." https://pressbooks.nscc.ca/worldhistory/chapter/the-hebrews/.

Oates, Harry. "The Maccabean Revolt." World History Encyclopedia, Oct. 29, 2015. https://www.worldhistory.org/article/827/the-maccabean-revolt/.

Ostberg, René. "Second Vatican Council." Encyclopedia Britannica, last modified Apr. 9, 2025. https://www.britannica.com/event/Second-Vatican-Council.

Oxford Reference. "Dominant Ideology." https://www.oxfordreference.com/display/10.1093/oi/authority.20110803095725846.

Parrinder, Geoffrey, ed. *World Religions: From Ancient History to the Present*. New York: Facts on File, 1971.

Partner, Peter. *God of Battles: Holy Wars of Christianity and Islam*. Princeton: Princeton University Press. 1997.

Paul VI. *Encyclical Letter: Humanae Vitae*. Vatican, July 25, 1968. https://www.vatican.va/content/paul-vi/en/encyclicals/documents/hf_p-vi_enc_25071968_humanae-vitae.html.

Pew Research Center. "About Three-in-Ten U.S. Adults Are Now Religiously Unaffiliated." Dec. 14, 2021. https://www.pewresearch.org/religion/2021/12/14/about-three-in-ten-u-s-adults-are-now-religiously-unaffiliated/.

Philosopher. "Biography: Muhammad." https://thephilosopher.net/muhammad/.

Pietz, Tim. "What Is Christian Fundamentalism? History and Meaning." Christianity, June 20, 2023. https://www.christianity.com/wiki/christian-terms/what-fundamentalist-history-meaning.html.

Pinnock, Clark, et al. *The Openness of God: A Biblical Challenge to the Traditional Understanding of God*. Downers Grove, IL: InterVarsity, 1994.

Plante, Thomas. "Religious and Spiritual Communities Must Adapt or Die: Surviving and Thriving During Challenging Contemporary Times." *Religions* 15 (2024) 791. https://www.mdpi.com/2077-1444/15/7/791.

Pluralism Project. "From Diversity to Pluralism." https://pluralism.org/from-diversity-to-pluralism.

Bibliography

Posner, Menachem. "A History of the Hebrew Monarchy." Chabad. https://www.chabad.org/library/article_cdo/aid/1935026/jewish/A-History-of-the-Hebrew-Monarchy.htm.

Presbyterian Church (U.S.A.). *Book of Order 2023-2025*. Part 2 of the Constitution of the Presbyterian Church (U.S.A.). Louisville: Office of the General Assembly, 2023. https://www.pcusa.org/sites/default/files/boo_final_large_print_2023-2025_v2.pdf.

Preston, Jesse Lee, et al. "Neuroscience and the Soul: Competing Explanations for the Human Experience." *Cognition* 127 (2013) 31–37. https://doi.org/10.1016/j.cognition.2012.12.003.

Priest, Stephen. "Quantum Physics and the Existence of God." *Religions* 15 (2024) 78. https://doi.org/10.3390/rel15010078.

Quranic Education. "Abu Bakr: The First Caliph." Quranic Studies Center, Dec. 3, 2023. https://quranicstudiescenter.com/abu-bakr-the-first-caliph/.

Räisänen, Heikki. "Tradition, Experience, Interpretation: A Dialectical Model for Describing the Development of Religious Thought." *Scripta Instituti Donneriani Aboensis* 17 (1999) 215–26. https://doi.org/10.30674/scripta.67255.

Rice, Richard. *The Future of Open Theism: From Antecedents to Opportunities*. Downers Grove, IL: InterVarsity, 2020.

Roach, David. "SBC May Tighten Faith Statement Amendment Process." Baptist Standard, Sept. 25, 2024. https://baptiststandard.com/news/baptists/sbc-may-tighten-faith-statement-amendment-process/.

Robbins, Jeffrey. *Radical Theology: A Vision for Change*. Bloomington: Indiana University Press, 2016.

Rorty, Richard, and Gianni Vattimo. *The Future of Religion*. New York: Columbia University Press, 2005.

Sanders, E. P. "St. Paul the Apostle." Encyclopedia Britannica, last modified Mar. 27, 2005. https://www.britannica.com/biography/Saint-Paul-the-Apostle.

Sanderson, Stephen. *Religious Evolution and the Axial Age*. London: Bloomsbury Academic, 2018.

Seaver, Carl. "The Thirty Years' War: Catholics vs. Protestants." History Defined. https://www.historydefined.net/thirty-years-war/.

Segal, Robert. *Myth: A Very Short Introduction*. Oxford: Oxford University Press, 2004.

Senz, Paul. "The Authority of Ecumenical Councils." Catholic Answers, Feb. 2, 2023. https://www.catholic.com/magazine/print-edition/the-authority-of-ecumenical-councils.

Shanes, Joshua. "Jewish Denominations: A Brief Guide for the Perplexed." Faith Counts. https://faithcounts.com/jewish-denominations-a-brief-guide-for-the-perplexed/.

Shelby, Alex. *The Evolution of Religion: How Religions Originate, Change, and Die*. Self-published, CreateSpace, 2014.

Bibliography

Singh, Bachitter. "Marx on Religion: The Opium of Masses." Pure Sociology, Nov. 23, 2024. https://puresociology.com/marx-on-religion-the-opium-of-masses/.

Sissa. "Is the Universe Designed for Life? A Bold New Experiment Aims to Find Out." SciTechDaily, Dec. 21, 2024. https://scitechdaily.com/is-the-universe-designed-for-life-a-bold-new-experiment-aims-to-find-out/.

Smietana, Robert. "As Organized Religion Falters, the Devil Falls on Hard Times." *Religion News Service*, July 27, 2023. https://religionnews.com/2023/07/27/as-organized-religion-falters-the-devil-falls-on-hard-times/.

Smith, Huston. *Why Religion Matters*. New York: HarperOne, 2001.

———. *The World's Religions*. San Francisco: HarperCollins, 1991.

Sociology Institute. "Auguste Comte's Law of Three Stages: The Evolutionary Stages of Society." Oct. 18, 2022. https://sociology.institute/sociological-theories-concepts/auguste-comte-law-three-stages-evolution-society/.

———. "The Process of Secularization and Its Impact." Feb. 7, 2023. https://sociology.institute/sociology-of-religion/marxian-theory-religion-oppression-instrument/.

Socratic Method. "Voltaire: 'If God Did Not Exist, It Would Be Necessary to Invent Him.'" https://www.socratic-method.com/quote-meanings-french/voltaire-if-god-did-not-exist-it-would-be-necessary-to-invent-him.

Sowerwine, James E. "Caliph and Caliphate." Oxford Bibliographies, last modified Dec. 14, 2009. https://www.oxfordbibliographies.com/display/document/obo-9780195390155/obo-9780195390155-0013.xml.

Stark, Rodney. *Discovering God: The Origins of the Great Religions and the Evolution of Belief*. New York: HarperOne, 2008.

Statistics and Data. "Major Religious Groups in the World." https://statisticsanddata.org/data/most-popular-religions-in-the-world-2025/.

Strand, Greg. "A Rationale for Amending Your Church's Statement of Faith." EFCA Strands of Thought, Feb. 18, 2020. https://blogs.efca.org/strands-of-thought/posts/a-rationale-for-amending-your-churchs-statement-of-faith.

Stringer, Martin. "Rethinking Animism: Thoughts from the Infancy of Our Discipline." *Journal of the Royal Anthropological Institute* 5 (1999) 541–55. https://www.jstor.org/stable/2661147.

StudyCorgi. "Sunni and Shia' Branches of Islam: The History of the Split." June 13, 2023. https://studycorgi.com/sunni-and-shia-branches-of-islam-the-history-of-the-split/.

Sullivan, Becky. "Pope Francis Approves Catholic Blessings for Same-Sex Couples, but Not for Marriage." NPR, Dec. 18, 2023. https://www.npr.org/2023/12/18/1220077102/pope-francis-blessings-same-sex-couples.

Sumit, Paul-Choudhury. "Tomorrow's Gods: What Is the Future of Religion?" *BBC*, Aug. 1, 2019. https://www.bbc.com/future/article/20190801-tomorrows-gods-what-is-the-future-of-religion.

Bibliography

Szocik, Konrad. "Critical Remarks on the Cognitive Science of Religion." *Zygon* 55 (2020) 157–84. https://doi.org/10.1111/zygo.12571.

———. "Religion and Religious Beliefs as Evolutionary Adaptations." *Zygon* 52 (2017) 24–52. https://www.zygonjournal.org/article/id/14374/.

This vs. That. "Deism vs. Theism." https://thisvsthat.io/deism-vs-theism.

Timmons, Greg. "Muhammad." Biography, Apr. 10, 2024. https://www.biography.com/religious-figures/muhammad.

Tuckness, Alex. "Locke's Political Philosophy." Stanford Encyclopedia of Philosophy, last modified Oct. 6, 2020. https://plato.stanford.edu/entries/locke-political/#Tole.

Unger, Roberto. *The Religion of the Future*. New York: Verso, 2014.

United Methodist Church. *The Book of Discipline of the United Methodist Church*. Nashville: United Methodist Publishing House, 2016. https://www.ctcumc.org/files/fileshare/2016-book-of-discipline.pdf.

United States Holocaust Memorial Museum. "Holocaust Survivors and the Establishment of the State of Israel (May 14, 1948)." Last modified Jan. 2, 2025. https://encyclopedia.ushmm.org/content/en/article/postwar-refugee-crisis-and-the-establishment-of-the-state-of-israel.

United States Office of the Historian. "The Arab-Israeli War of 1948." https://history.state.gov/milestones/1945-1952/arab-israeli-war.

Van Eyghen, Hans. "Animism and Science." *Religions* 14 (2023) 653. https://doi.org/10.3390/rel14050653.

Viney, Donald. "Process Theism." Stanford Encyclopedia of Philosophy, last modified June 4, 2002. https://plato.stanford.edu/archives/sum2022/entries/process-theism/.

Washington Post. "Nearly Half of Americans Think U.S. Should Be 'Christian Nation,' Poll Finds." Oct. 27, 2022. https://www.washingtonpost.com/religion/2022/10/27/america-christian-nation-pew-nationalism/.

Weidenkopf, Steve. "The Protestants Who Came Before the Protestants." Catholic Answers, Aug. 26, 2022. https://www.catholic.com/magazine/online-edition/the-protestants-who-came-before-the-protestants.

Wein, Berel. "The End of the Hasmoneans, the Rise of Rome." Jewish History. https://www.jewishhistory.org/end-of-hasmoneans-rise-of-rome-4/.

Welker, Christopher. "Habermas and Ratzinger on the Future of Religion." *Scottish Journal of Theology* 63 (2010) 456–73. https://doi.org/10.1017/S0036930610000517.

White, Andrew D. *History of the Warfare of Science with Theology and Christendom*. New York: MacMillan, 1897; Project Gutenberg, 2009. https://www.gutenberg.org/files/505/505-h/505-h.htm.

Whitehead, Alfred North. *Religion in the Making: Lowell Lectures, 1926*. New York: Fordham University Press, 1996.

Who Is Hussain. "The Full Story of Hussain." https://whoishussain.org/who-is-hussain/the-full-story/.

Bibliography

Wittberg, Patricia. "Generational Change in Religion and Religious Practice." *Review of Religious Research* 63 (2021) 461–82. https://doi.org/10.1007/s13644-021-00455-0.

Wood, W. Jay. *God*. Montreal: McGill-Queens University Press, 2014.

World History Edu. "Abu Bakr: The First Caliph and Father-in-Law of the Prophet Muhammad." Dec. 13, 2024. https://worldhistoryedu.com/abu-bakr-the-first-caliph.

———."Ancient Israel and Judah." Dec. 10, 2024. https://worldhistoryedu.com/ancient-israel-and-judah/.

———. "The Edict of Thessalonica in 380." Jan. 30, 2025. https://worldhistoryedu.com/the-edict-of-thessalonica-in-380/.

———. "Mernaptah Stele." Dec. 9, 2024. https://worldhistoryedu.com/merneptah-stele/.

———. "What Was the Fatimid Caliphate?" Oct. 11, 2024. https://worldhistoryedu.com/what-was-the-fatimid-caliphate-history-major-facts/.

World Religions. "Shintoism." https://worldreligions.wordpress.ncsu.edu/shintoism/.

Wright, Ellen G. "An Era of Spiritual Darkness." In *The Great Controversy*, 49–60. Mountain View, CA: Pacific Press, 1911. https://m.egwwritings.org/en/book/132.200.

Wright, Robert. *The Evolution of God*. New York: Little, Brown, 2009.

Zuckerman, Phil. "Why Education Corrodes Religious Faith." *Psychology Today*, Nov. 3, 2014. https://www.psychologytoday.com/us/blog/the-secular-life/201411/why-education-corrodes-religious-faith.

Index

Abbas ibn Abd al-Muttalib, 25
Abdullah ibn Abd al-Muttalib, 19
Abd al-Rahman I, 26
Abraham, 6, 10, 19
Abu Bakr, 22, 23
Abu Talib, 19, 20
Adaptationist Approach, 66, 67
Afghanistan, 26, 28
Africa
   North, 14
   Sub-Saharan, 36
Aggiornamento, 37
Agnostic, 85, 86
Alhambra Decree, 14
Ali ibn Abi Talib, 22, 23
Alexandria, 14
   Treaty of, 14
American Sociological Association, 55
Amina bint Wahb, 19
Animism, 4
Anthropic Principle, 78
Apollonius of Tyana, 68
Arabian Peninsula, 21, 22
Armstrong, Karen, 4, 29, 49, 50, 60, 61, 72, 84, 85, 88
Asia, 5, 30, 36, 92
Aslan, Reza, 2, 4, 7, 23, 31
Assyria, 12, 16
Atheists, 76, 85, 90
Augustine of Hippo, 68
Ayatollah, 29

Azerbaijan, 25

Babylonian, 12, 16, 17
Baghdad, 26
Bahrain, 25
Bar Kokhba Revolt, 14
Battle, 24
   Ain Jalut, 27
   Homs, 27
   Karbala, 24
   Nahrawa, 24
Bellah, Robert, 1, 3, 5, 11, 17, 93
Bible, 6, 7, 36, 68, 69, 94–96
   Hebrew, 5, 6, 16–18, 30
   New Testament, 5, 6, 31
   Old Testament, 5, 6
Big Bang, 77–79
Biology, 45, 59, 74–77, 83, 84
Black Death, 27
Books of the Bible
   Exodus, 6, 16, 96
   Genesis, 6, 16
   Leviticus, 16, 94
   Numbers, 16
   Revelation, 31
Buddhism, 60, 65, 82
Bussey, Peter, 77, 79–81

Caliph, 22–24, 26
Caliphate, 23, 26
   Abbasid, 26, 27
   Cordoba, 26
   Umayyad, 25

Index

Calvinist, 48, 56
Campbell, Doug, 46
Canaan, 9–12
Canon, 31, 32, 37
Caputo, John, 50, 51, 71, 93
Carroll, Sean, 82
Cathars, 98
Catholicism, 32, 36, 37, 40, 42, 44, 63, 98
Chaldea, 16
   Chaldeans, 6
China, 27, 87
Chopra, Deepak, 68
Christianity, xv, xvi, 30–37
Church, xii, xvi, 3, 32, 37, 38, 46, 55, 56, 59, 60, 62, 70–73, 84, 91–93
   Catholic, 33, 35, 37, 39, 44, 45, 92
   Christian, 31, 40
   Eastern, 31
   Episcopal, 70
   Evangelical, 40, 70, 71
   Latin, 31, 33
   Lutheran, 41
   Morman, 36, 40
   Orthodox, 32
   Protestant, 32
   Presbyterian, 41, 70
   United Church, of Christ, 70
   United Methodist, 41
Cognitive, 65–67
   Capacities, 65
   Science of Religion (CSR), 65
Communism, 87
Communist Manifesto, 87
Comte, Auguste, 50, 61
Constantine I, 31
Constitution on the Sacred Liturgy, 39
Conway, Daniel, 51
Coogan, Michael, 5
Councils, 31–33, 37, 38, 45
   Constantinople, 33
   Ephesus, 33

First Vatican, xvi
   Nicaea, 33
   Second, Vatican, 39, 44
Consciousness, 79, 81, 102
   Neural Correlates, 82
Cootsona, Greg, 88
Crusades, 33–36, 91, 92
Curie, Marie, 77
Cyprus, 34
Cyrus the Great, 12, 17

Damascus, 26, 30
Dante, 6
Darwin, 75
David, 12
Dawkins, Richard, 59, 68, 75, 76, 78, 90
Deism, 59, 65
Deity, 2, 65, 76, 87, 88, 94, 99
Devil, 71, 83
Diet of Worms, 35
Doctrine, xv, xvi, 5, 7, 29, 32, 36–41, 45, 46, 49, 65, 82, 98
   Infallibility, 32
   Trinitarian, 33
Durkheim, Emile, 55, 56, 84
Dynasty, 35
   Abbasid, 25, 26
   Fatimid, 14, 27
   Ghaznavid, 26
   Hasmonean, 14
   Saffarid, 26
   Saminid, 26
   Tahirid, 26
   Umayyad, 24

Edicts, 36
   Milan, 31
   Thessalonica, 31
Egypt, 5, 6, 9–11, 14, 23, 27, 33
Einstein, Albert, 77
Empires
   Abbasid, 26
   Akkadia, 9
   Babylonian, 12, 17

Index

Byzantine, 26
Islamic, 33-34, 38
Mongol, 26, 27
Muslim, 23, 27, 43
Neo-Assyrian, 12
Ottoman, 15
Persian, 12
Roman, 31-33, 68
Samanid, 38
Seleucid, 13
Seljuk, 26
Sumer, 9
Umayyad, 24, 25
Encyclicals, 38
Epic of Gilgamesh, 5, 6
Eucharist, 98
Europe, 3, 5, 15, 27, 28, 31, 33-36, 43
   Central, 14
   Eastern, 14, 28
   Northeastern, 34
   Western, 35
Evangelicals, 99
Evely, Bob, 33
Ezra, 17

fMRI, 82
Fundamentalism, 37
   Christian, 36, 65
   Islamic, 28, 29

Gabriel, 19, 20
Ghazan, Mahmud, 27
Gemara, 17
Genesis, 6
Gentiles, 30, 31
Georgians, 33
Germany, 15
Gould, Stephen Jay, 59
Grady, Monica, 78, 83
Great Assembly, 17
Great Synagogue, 17
Greek, 5, 7, 13, 16, 33, 92, 99

Habermas, Jürgen, 61
Hadith, 29

Hadrian, 14
Halal, 97
Hamas, 42
Haram, 97
Hasan ibn Ali, 24
Hashim family, 19
Hawking, Stephen, 77, 80, 83
Heaven, xvi, 6, 7, 18, 30, 71, 83, 87, 90, 91
Hebrews, 9, 11, 16
Hell, 6, 83, 84, 90, 91
Heraclius I, 14
Hezbollah, 42
Hinduism, xi, 60, 82, 92
Hira, 20
Hitler, Adolph, 15
Holocaust, 15
Hope, xi, 2, 58, 68, 73, 86, 89
Houthis, 42
Hus, Jan, 35
Hussain ibn Ali, 24

Ihm, Elliott, 89
Ijtihad, 28, 29
India, 5
Indian, 92
Intelligent Design, xii, 77, 78
Internet, xv, 70, 88
Iran, 25, 29, 42, 43
Isaac, 6, 10
Islam, xi, xv, xvi, 19-23, 27-29, 35, 37, 43, 52, 60, 81, 97, 99
Israel, 9, 10, 12, 13, 15, 17, 42, 43
Italy, 34

Jacob, 10, 11
Jerusalem, 12-14, 17, 27, 30
Jesus Christ, xvi, 6, 7, 19, 30, 31, 36, 40, 45-47, 68, 70, 82, 87, 88, 92
Jews, 9-11, 13-15, 30, 42, 94, 95
Judah, 9, 12, 13, 17
Judaism, xi, xv, xvi, 9, 16-18

Kami, 4

Index

Kardong, Kenneth, 2, 3, 64, 73, 76, 92, 94, 96
Karma, 89, 91
Khamenei, Sayyid Ali, 29
Killen, Patricia, 39
King Philip IV, 92
Kingdom
   God, 47, 72, 83, 84, 90
   Israel, 9, 12, 13, 17
   Judah, 9, 12, 13, 17
Knight, Christopher, 45, 49
Knights Templar, 92
Kristof, Nicholas, 70
Kuwait, 28

Latin America, 36
Lebanon, 24, 28
Levant, 9, 27, 34
Luther, Martin, 35, 36, 46
Lutherans, 99

Maccabees, 13
   Maccabean Revolt, 13
Magdalene, Mary, 45
Malchus, 68
Malta, 34
Mamluk, 27
Marx, Karl, 56, 57, 87
Mawali, 25
Mead, George, 57, 58
Mecca, 19–21
Medina, 19–21, 24
Merneptah Stele, 9, 10
Mesopotamia, 5, 6
Messiah, 30
Methodists, 99
Middle East, 5, 11, 26, 27, 94, 99
Miracle, 68, 69
Mishnah, 17
Mlodinow, Leonard, 80
Moksha, 82
De Molay, Jacques, 92
Mount Sinai, 11, 17
Moses, 6, 11, 16, 19, 70
Mostert, Christiaan, 47

Mozumder, Muhammad Golam Nabi, 61
Muawiyah I, 24
Muhammad, 19–25, 29, 68
Mutahid, 29
Myths, 1, 4–8, 11, 16–18, 50, 87

Nazis, 15
Nestorius, 33
Neuroscience, 82
Newton, Isaac, 77
Nicene Creed, 33
Nietzsche, Friedrich, 50
Ninety-five Theses, 35
Nones, 85, 86, 101
Norelius, Per-Johan, 65

Occam's razor, 75, 76
Open Theism, 46–49
Osama Bin Laden, 28, 29

Palestine, 15
Papal Bull, 37, 38
Paul, the Apostle, 30, 31, 46, 87
Pentateuch, 16
Pentecostal, 65
Persia, 23, 26
Persistence, 59, 63, 64, 73, 84, 94
Peter, xvi
   Primacy of, xvi
Physics, xii, 45, 77, 79–81, 83, 84, 101
Pinnock, Clark, 48
Pluralism, 59, 62
Popes, xvi, 22, 31, 36–38, 40, 44, 91, 98, 99
   Benedict XIV, 38
   Clement V, 92
   Francis, 38
   John XXIII, 37
   Leo X, 36
   Paul VI, 38
   Pius XII, 38
Positivists, 49, 50
Post-Secularism, 60, 61
Presentists, 49

Index

Priest, Stephen, 81
Primacy of Peter, xvi
Protestant, 3, 35, 36, 40, 48, 56, 70, 71, 85, 99

Al-Qaeda, 28
Quantum, 81, 82
   Field Theory, 82
   Physics, 81
Quraysh, 19, 23
Qur'an, 22, 23, 28, 29,

Reformation, 35, 48
Reinterpretation, 59, 63
Rice, Richard, 49
Ridda Wars, 22
Rome, xvi, 31
   Romans, 14
Rorty, Richard, 51, 93

Sacrosanctum Concilium, 39
Samsara, 82
Samuel, 11, 12
Sanderson, Stephen, 7, 11, 23, 91
Saudi Arabia, 28
Saul of Tarsus, 30
Schism, 22, 35
   East-West (Great), 33, 34
Secularization, xii, 58–61
Shelby, Alex, 7, 85, 86, 99
Shia, 14, 23–26, 28, 29, 43
Shinto, xi, 4, 92
   State, 92
Simon, 13
Sicily, 34
Sistine Chapel, 89
Smedes, Taede, 66
Smith, Huston, 2
Socialization, 56, 57, 63, 76
Sociology, xi, xii, 1–3, 8, 45, 55–59, 61, 64, 65, 69, 72–74, 83, 84
Solomon, 12
Soul, 53, 66, 81–84, 90
Soulmate, 89
Southern Baptists, 40
Soviet Union, 15, 69, 87

Spirit, xv, 4, 30, 50, 66, 82
   Holy, 7, 33, 46
Stark, Rodney, xv, 3, 5, 8, 49, 74, 98, 99
Sultanate
   Ayyubid, 27
   Mamluk, 27
Sunnah, 29
Sunni, 21–26, 28, 43
Supernatural, 4, 6, 39, 50, 86, 87, 96
Syria, 9, 22–24, 28, 33, 43
Szocik, Konrad, 67

Taliban, 28
Talmud, 17, 18
   Babylonian, 17
   Jerusalem, 17
Tanakh, 16
Temple, 12
   First, 12
   Mount, 14
   Second, 12
Theodosius I, 31, 33
Theology, xi, xii, xv, 2, 45–53, 63, 66, 83, 88
   Positivist, 49
   Process, 52
   Radical, 51, 52
Torah, 11, 16–18, 95
Traditions, xii, 16, 17, 21, 26, 28, 32, 37, 46–48, 55, 60, 62–66, 70, 71, 81, 94–96
Turks, 26

Ubi Primum, 38
Umar ibn al-Khattab, 22
Umayyads, 24–26
United Nations, 15
   Educational, Scientific, and Cultural Organization, 69
   General Assembly, 15
United States, 15, 28, 45, 60, 68, 69, 87, 90
Uthman ibn Affan, 23

Van Elk, Michiel, 89

Index

Vatican, 37
Vatican Councils, 37
   First, xvi
   Second, 37, 39, 44
Vattimo, Gianni, 51, 93
Voltaire, 7

Weber, Max, 56
White, Andrew, 16
Whitehead, Alfred, 1, 4, 93
Wood, W. Jay, 8, 46

World Trade Center, 28
Wright, Robert, 62, 73, 77, 81, 83, 93
Wycliffe, John, 35

Yahweh, 8, 11, 17, 18, 43, 92

Zealot, 14
Zion, 12
Zoroastrians, 23
Zwingli, Ulrich, 35

About the Author

Stephen Schwalbe is an adjunct professor at Columbia College. Formerly, he was a professor at the Air War College and American Public University. During his thirty-four years in the U.S. Air Force, he served as the Assistant Defense Intelligence Officer for the Middle East and Terrorism, Air Attache to South Korea, Air Attache to Jordan, and Inspection Director for the Department of Defense Inspector General.

www.ingramcontent.com/pod-product-compliance
Lightning Source LLC
Chambersburg PA
CBHW050831160426
43192CB00010B/1976